Giants and Warriors

Giants and Warriors

Legends of Ancient Greece retold by
JAMES REEVES

Illustrated by Sarah Nechamkin

Blackie: Glasgow and London

Blackie & Son Limited
Bishopbriggs, Glasgow G64 2NZ
450/452 Edgware Road, London W2 1EG

ISBN 0 216 90444 7 (paper)
ISBN 0 216 90446 3 (cased)

Printed in Great Britain by
Robert MacLehose and Company Limited
Printers to the University of Glasgow

Contents

Giants and Warriors

Introduction

In this book you will read some of the world's greatest folk tales. A folk tale is one which has come down to us from the lips of the 'folk' - that is, the common people of any land; it is anonymous - it has, that is to say, no known original author, whoever may have chosen to write it down later; it is also widespread, appearing in different forms in different countries. The folk tales of Ancient Greece - some of them older than the work of one of the greatest of all poets, Homer, who is thought to have lived about a thousand years before Christianity - are among those which have charmed and delighted people for many centuries, because of their variety, their magic, their vigour, their excitement and their poetic treatment of man and nature.

Now the Greeks have always been noted for their enquiring minds. They had the virtue of curiosity, which, as Dr Johnson said, 'is, in great and generous minds, the first passion and the last'. Had it not been for the enquiring mind of Greece, western Europe would have known little progress, and we should have been without some of our finest stories, our greatest plays and our most beautiful poetry. These ancient Greeks looked at the world around them and wondered how it came to be as it is. They gradually invented and passed on to their children a vast body of tradition about the nature of men, women and animals, about the beginnings of the natural world and the monsters that inhabited it, and, above all, about the gods who ruled the world of men. The gods were all-important to the Greeks. Invisibly they reigned in the upper air or on mountain tops, especially that of Mount Olympus, coming down to earth sometimes in disguise to alter or supervise the lives of men. The idea of one god only is a Jewish and, later, a Christian one. The Greeks had many gods, each responsible for a different part of the earth or a different department in human affairs. The belief in the existence of these gods explained the facts of nature as they presented themselves to the imagination of the Greeks. Thus Zeus, the chief of all the gods, was the cause of thunder and lightning. Poseidon ruled the seas, and Hades, or Dis, the underworld, to which all must go when they die. The troubles of men arose from one of two causes: either they did wrong and angered the gods, or the gods quarrelled among themselves, and their quarrels were reflected in war or famine or some other disaster on earth. In the same way, happiness and good fortune came to men because the gods were pleased and willed it so.

The gods had the same passions and weaknesses as men. Because of the Sun god Apollo's desire to possess the maiden Daphne, who did not love him, she ran from him and escaped him, just as he was catching up with her, by turning into a laurel tree. This tale charmingly and satisfyingly explained the origin of one of the trees found growing in the land of the Greeks. What was the beginning of those faults and weaknesses of men - anger, greed, jealousy, spite, cruelty and the rest - by which so much trouble and misery is caused? The Greeks had the delightful idea that at some former time - a lost golden age - all these things were shut up in a box, which it was forbidden to open; but Pandora, carried away by her foolish inquisitiveness, in reckless disobedience lifted the lid. Instantly all the evils in the box escaped and have never been recaptured since. We may smile at some of these folk tales, but we must admire their combination of simplicity and ingenuity.

Not all the legends of the Greeks were about nature or the quarrels and loves of the gods. Some of the best were about ancient heroes, such as Perseus or Jason or Heracles. Their heroic deeds were recounted in songs and stories, growing and changing as they were handed down, age after age. These heroes, or demigods, probably had historical originals, though many miraculous and superhuman actions were woven into their legends, so that we can no longer say what was true and what was invented.

It would take too long to describe here the world of the Greeks and their marvellous tales. The stories can be enjoyed for themselves, without the scholar's knowledge of their meaning and origins. But some readers may wonder how they came down to us. They came first from the ancient Greek poets, Homer and Hesiod, from later poets such as Pindar, and from scholars and collectors such as Diodorus. One very important source is the writings of the Roman poet Ovid, and it is from his poems that many of our later versions come. The Romans had no true mythology themselves, only a rather vague worship of the spirits of nature, of agriculture and husbandry. But when they conquered Greece, they were as delighted with the folklore they found as anyone has been later. They took over the Greek gods and worshipped them under names of their own; thus the Greek goddess of love, Aphrodite, became Venus; the leader of the gods, Zeus, became Jupiter or Jove; the hero Heracles was known to the Romans as Hercules. Through the Romans, then, much that might have been lost of Greek mythology has survived, to entertain and astonish readers in all lands for the past two thousand years.

One other feature of this book remains to be mentioned. English readers, since the days when Greek used to be taught in most schools, find difficulty in pronouncing the names of Greek gods, heroes or places. A guide to the pronunciation of these names is given at the beginning of this book, and where the Romans had different forms of these names, these are also given. This guide is worth studying, for it will surely be agreed that the stories sound better if Penelope, Persephone or Telemachus are read as they should be and not turned into English-sounding names.

J.R.
Lewes, 1969

Pronunciation Guide

Roman equivalents of Greek names are given in brackets.
AE = EE (as in KEEP); CH = K; PH = F
C is hard (as in CAT) except where marked thus: AÇIS
Ȳ long (as in SKY) Y̆ short (as in MYTH)
Other vowels short unless marked thus: ACHILLĒS

Abdē'ra

Absyr'tus

Achi'llēs

Ā'çis

Acri'sius

Admē'tus

Aeāē'a

Aegē'an

Ae'gēus

Ae'olus

Ae'son

Ae'tēs

Ae'thra

Alçi'nous

Alcmē'nē

Alçȳ'onē

Alphē'us

A'my̆cus

Amy̆mō'nē

Androm'eda

Anti'nous

Aphrodī'tē (Venus)

Apo'llō

Ā'rēs (Mars)

Arethū'sa

Ar'gonauts

Aria'dne

Ari'on

Art'emis (Diana)

Asclē'pius

Atalan'ta

Ath'amas

Athē'nē (Minerva)

Augē'as

Auto'ly̆cus

Bria'reus

Ca'lāis

Calli'ope

Caly̆'pso

Cassiopē'ia

Melan'thius

Menelā'us

Mĭ'das

Mĭ'nos

Mĭ'notaur

Mor'phēus

Mycē'nae

Nausicā'a

Nemē'a

Nephē'le

Nē'reïds

Nē'rēus

Odў'ssēus (Ulysses)

Olўm'pus

Or'phēus

Pactō'lus

Pallā'dium

Pandor'a

Parnas'sus

Pasi'phaē

Peg'asus

Pe'lias

Penel'opē

Pēnē'us

Per'dix

Perian'der

Perse'phonē

Per'sēus

Phaeā'cians

Phā'eton

Philē'mon

Phĭ'nēus

Phrix'us

Phrў'gia

Polўdec'tēs

Polўdēū'cēs (Pollux)

Polўphē'mus

Posei'don (Neptune)

Prĭ'am

Procrus'tēs

Promē'thēus

Psȳ'chē

Sche'ria

Scĭ'ron

Scўl'la

Se'riphos

Sīlē'nus

Si'nis

Si'non

Si'sўphus

Stўgian

Stўmphā'lus

Stўx

Symplē'gadēs

Sȳ'rinx

Tan'talus

Tele'machus

Ten'edos

Thēb(e)s

Thē'sēus

Thes'salў

Ti'rўns

Tĭ'tans

Tmō'lus

Troi'zen

Tȳ'phōn (Typhoeus)

Zeph'ўrus

Zē'tēs

Zeūs (Jupiter *or* Jove)

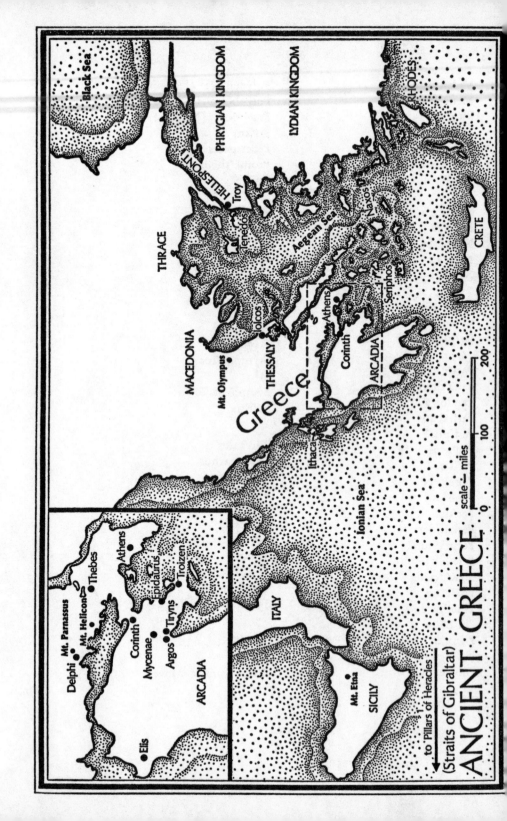

ANCIENT GREECE
(Straits of Gibraltar)
to Pillars of Heracles

scale — miles
0   100   200

Black Sea

PHRYGIAN KINGDOM

LYDIAN KINGDOM

RHODES

HELLESPONT

Troy
Tenedos

THRACE

Aegean sea

Naxos

Seriphos

CRETE

MACEDONIA

Iolcos

Athens

Corinth

ARCADIA

Mt. Olympus

THESSALY

Greece

Ithaca

Ionian Sea

ITALY

Mt. Etna

SICILY

Delphi
Mt. Parnassus
Mt. Helicon

Thebes

Athens

Epidaurus

Troizen

Corinth
Mycenae
Argos
Tiryns

ARCADIA

Elis

Baucis and Philemon

On a hill in the country of Phrygia stand two trees, an oak and a lime, so close together that their trunks are intertwined. Near them is a lake where now only the birds live. Long, long ago a flourishing city stood there. This is the story of how the city became a lake, and the two trees grew together, side by side.

One day Zeus, father of the gods, and his son Hermes travelled through Phrygia, disguising themselves as poor men, in order to see how kind the people of that country were to strangers. From door to door they went, seeking shelter for the night, but not a door was opened to them. The richer the house, the meaner was their reception.

'It is too late,' the voices said from behind barred doors. 'Be on your way. We have no room for strangers.'

'It is near nightfall,' another voice would say. 'Be off with you. We want no tramps and beggars here.'

Zeus and Hermes trudged on. At last, just as they were at the point of despair, they found a tiny thatched cottage on the outskirts of the city, whose door was opened at their knock. It was the home of two old people, Philemon and his wife Baucis. They were very poor, but managed to make ends meet by thrift and the kindness of their hearts. In the houses of the rich you will find masters and servants. In the cottage of Philemon and Baucis there was no master and no servant. Both were masters and both served each other.

As soon as the two gods bent their heads to enter the low doorway, the old man brought forward a bench for them to rest on, and his wife threw upon it an old rug made of sheepskin, worn and tattered with age. Then Baucis raked out the ashes of the fire and threw on dried leaves and bark. Bending low before the fire, she blew upon it and kindled the dying embers into flames. She threw some sticks on the fire and put on an old cooking pot full of water. Philemon brought in vegetables and herbs from the garden, and Baucis cut them up and put them in the pot. The old man took down a side of smoked ham from the beam above the chimney, cut off slices of the meat and put them in the pot

with the herbs and vegetables. Then, while the meal was heating, Philemon gave his guests a bowl of water to wash in, asking them politely about their journey and the road they had come by.

Next Baucis, with trembling hands, placed a rickety table before the travellers, wiped its worn surface with sweet-smelling herbs and placed upon it some olives in a wooden bowl. Beside this she laid some cheese and a salad in dishes of cracked earthenware, the best she had in her cupboard. Then she found wooden cups and a pitcher of clear water. Her husband brought out a little wine, which he poured into a bowl for the entertainment of the travellers. The steaming dish of meat and vegetables was soon ready, and this was put on the table. Baucis, in her ancient, trembling voice, bade the guests welcome, and urged them to eat and drink.

Zeus and Hermes, delighted with their welcome, began to eat of the food and drink of the wine and water, while Philemon and Baucis chatted to them of this and that, stopping from time to time to put more sticks on the fire or serve them with cheese and salad. As the meal went on, the old folks were disturbed to see that, as soon as the wine bowl began to be emptied, it was refilled as if by magic. There had been little enough wine to start with, but now it seemed as if there was a never-ending stream. It was this which made Philemon and Baucis realise that they were entertaining gods. How else was the endless supply of wine to be explained? Looking into the faces of their guests, they could now see that they were indeed no mere men, but immortals from heaven. So they fell upon their knees before Zeus and Hermes and begged them to grant pardon for their humble entertainment.

Then the old couple put their heads together and considered how they might offer something worthier of their divine guests. Waddling about the doorway of their cottage was a goose, ancient but stately, which they kept as a guardian of their household. It had at least enough strength to cackle when danger approached. They made up their minds to sacrifice the goose in honour of their guests. They would capture it, wring its neck, pluck it and get it ready for the pot. This at least would be better than the smoked ham and vegetables which was the best they had been able to offer.

But the goose refused to have anything to do with the old people's plan. It fled from them, ran round the cottage, squawking indignantly, and finally sheltered on the floor between the feet of the gods. Zeus forbade the old people to kill it, saying:

'Spare the goose, my friends, guardian of your household. You have feasted us well, and we have no need of it. We are

gods, and everywhere but in your cottage we have been treated with meanness and inhospitality. We must repay the inhabitants of this land as they have served us, but we will protect you. Leave your house and come with us to the top of that hill. Do as we bid.'

The gods arose from their bench and led the way up the hill. Philemon and Baucis obeyed. Each with a staff in hand, they hobbled and panted up the hill behind their guests. It was now night, but the sky was bright with stars. Turning round, they saw by the light of the stars that a great water had risen and covered all the city behind them, except only their tiny cottage. It alone was left standing above the flood. The old couple, breathing hard after their efforts to climb the hill, gazed upon the scene, wringing their hands and lamenting the fate of their neighbours, whose houses had been swallowed up in the rising water. Then they saw a marvel. For their cottage was transformed by divine magic into a temple. Its creaking posts and weathered walls were turned into columns of stone. Its thatched roof became pure gold. Its floor was paved with marble.

Zeus spoke kindly to the old couple.

'You have given the gods a welcome where others barred their doors,' he said. 'We have saved you from destruction, and your cottage has been turned into a temple fit for the worship of the gods. What request will you make us? Whatever you desire shall be granted you.'

Philemon and Baucis mumbled together. It did not take them long to make up their minds.

'We ask,' said Philemon in his old, quavering voice, 'to be allowed to spend the rest of our lives as guardians of the temple that was our home. Here we have lived, and here we will die together when our time comes. We wish to be allowed to die at the same moment, so that my wife may not live to see my funeral nor I ever behold her grave.'

Their request was granted. For the rest of their lives they were the priests of the temple, keeping it clean and accepting the sacrifices of pious travellers, sweeping its floor and setting fresh herbs upon the altar.

Then one day, when they were very old indeed, they stood together before the temple. As they talked quietly together of old times, a chill wind blew. They both shivered, and Baucis saw Philemon begin to grow leaves. Philemon saw his wife changing in the same way. They felt themselves rooted to the ground. Leaves grew about their heads, and they soon knew that they were becoming trees. They bade farewell to each other, but neither felt sad. They had lived long and were tired. They had been together as long as they could remember, and even death was not to separate them. Bark had grown up around their old limbs.

'Good-bye, dear wife,' said Philemon.

'Good-bye, my husband,' sighed Baucis with her last breath, and the bark closed silently over their mouths.

The man had become an oak, and the woman a lime-tree.

For many years the Phrygian shepherds showed the two trees to their children and grandchildren, telling them the story of the old people whose kindness to strangers had earned them the reward of being together for ever. As the years went by, they grew closer even than they had been in life. Their trunks and their boughs were twisted together, so that it was hard to say which was which.

Eros and Psyche

Psyche was the youngest daughter of a king and queen. Her two elder sisters were more than commonly beautiful, but Psyche's loveliness was such that strangers drew in their breath when they saw her. She was slender and graceful; her hair hung in soft coils about her shoulders; her gestures and movements, her voice and her smile, were full of charm and sweetness. But it was the beauty of her face, above all, which attracted every gazer. The blue depths of her eyes, despite a certain mournfulness, seemed to smile with a faraway look, as if she were dreaming of things outside this world. So great was the fame of Psyche's beauty that people came from distant lands only to look at her. They said she was lovelier even than Aphrodite herself, queen and goddess of beauty.

Gradually men began to forsake the altars of Aphrodite and pay devotion only to Psyche. They strewed flowers in her path and offered up prayers to the young princess. When the news of this reached Aphrodite, she was incensed with anger. What was the use of having been proclaimed goddess of beauty if a mere mortal was to be worshipped as if she were divine?

'I will be revenged on this impudent girl,' she cried. 'I will make her sorry for her extraordinary powers of attraction.'

The son of Aphrodite was a young man of unusual beauty named Eros. In some regions he was worshipped as the god of love, though indeed it was Aphrodite herself who should have been so regarded. Eros roamed the earth with a bow and a quiver full of arrows, and if he aimed at a mortal in the presence of another of the opposite sex, instantly his victim fell in love. Sometimes Eros was regarded as being blindfolded, so that his arrows fell haphazard. If he were nearby, any man or woman might instantly fall in love with anyone else, for no apparent reason whatsoever. Sometimes Eros used his power with kindliness and foresight, sometimes blindly and for sheer mischief.

In her anger against poor Psyche, Aphrodite sent for her son.

'Go and find that wretched young woman,' she told him, 'and make her fall in love with some hideous creature. In this way she will be punished for her presumption.'

In the garden of Aphrodite were two fountains, one of sweet water, the other of bitter. Eros took from each a tiny bottle and with these he hastened to Psyche's room in her father's palace. Here he found her asleep, and from the bottle of bitter water he sprinkled a few drops on her lips. At once Psyche awoke and opened her eyes. Eros was invisible. But in that instant he fell in love with her, so overcome was he by her beauty. He was full of sorrow at what he had done, and tried to undo it by sprinkling her hair with the sweet water from the other bottle. Thus Psyche felt both joy and bitterness, delighting in her beauty but sorrowing because it seemed to make all men afraid of her. For Aphrodite, goddess of love, was her enemy and her beauty brought her no happiness. Everyone admired her; everyone spoke her praises; but no prince nor king nor commoner sought her hand in marriage. They were afraid to court one whom all united in worshipping. It was as if she were above even

8

kings. Her two sisters, more moderate in charms, had both found husbands among neighbouring princes; but Psyche alone sat brooding in her room, hating the very perfection of beauty which brought her only flattery but no love.

The girl's unhappy state alarmed her father and mother. They feared they had in some way offended against the gods, so they sought the advice of the oracle – the answer given by a priest or priestess to those who ask what they must do. They went to see the priest of Apollo in his temple at Delphi and asked what they should do.

Sternly the oracle replied:

'Your daughter is not meant to be the wife of any mortal lover. She is destined by the gods to be the bride of a monster whom neither gods nor men can resist. He dwells upon the top of a mountain, and thither your daughter must go and seek him.'

When these terrible words were known, all the people were horrified. Some wept and some tore their hair. The king and queen were almost out of their minds. But poor Psyche took the news more calmly.

'My dear parents,' she said quietly, 'you grieve now; yet before, when the people greeted me as a goddess, you rejoiced. You should have grieved then, and so you would have been ready for this cruel oracle. I am resigned to my fate. Lead me to it.'

So a procession wound slowly up the pine-covered slopes of the mountain, and on the top of it Psyche was left alone.

For a long time the princess stood on the summit of the mountain. Chill winds blowing across the stony wastes made her gather her robe tightly about her. She began to feel afraid, and tears filled her lovely eyes.

'What have I done to deserve such a fate as this?' she asked herself in anguish. 'Was it my fault that all men called me beautiful and forsook the altars of Aphrodite?'

Then, as if in answer to her words of sorrow, the wind
changed, and Zephyrus, blowing strong and warm from the
west, lifted the girl in his arms and carried her gently down
the mountain into a flowery vale, full of sweet perfumes and
the murmur of birds among the summer leaves. Here
Psyche lay down beside a rippling stream and fell fast asleep.

When she awoke, she found herself near a grove of
stately trees surrounding a pleasant spring of pure water.
Into this grove she strayed, and before long she was standing
in front of a delightful palace. It seemed to have been designed
and built, not by men, but by some god. She entered the
palace and wandered through its stately apartments, mar-
velling at the golden pillars supporting the carved roof, the
elaborate paintings of gods and hunting scenes which
adorned the walls. There were carvings and sculptures,

jewelled objects of rare worth, and many other treasures to captivate the eye.

As she was gazing at a richly embroidered screen, Psyche was surprised to hear a voice, though no one was in sight.

'Fair queen,' said the voice, 'this palace is yours and all that it contains. We whose voices you hear are your servants, and we will obey your every command. Go to your own apartment and rest on the bed. Afterwards you will find your bath prepared, and nearby you will find a table on which will be food and wine for your refreshment. If you will be pleased to partake of these things, we will be in attendance to see that you lack nothing.'

After she had rested and bathed, Psyche sat down to enjoy the delicious meal which appeared as if by magic. As she ate and drank, her ears were feasted on the music of hidden instruments, ravishingly sweet and harmonious. She began to forget her fears and even the fate that awaited her.

She had not yet seen her future husband – the cruel monster to whom she had been promised. But he came at night and left her before the hours of darkness had passed. She was surprised to find that he spoke to her, not in fierce and threatening tones, but only in words of love and admiration. She longed to see him, but he would not let her.

'It is better,' the gentle voice told her, 'that I should remain unseen. I beg you not to ask to see my face. I love and cherish you, dear Psyche, and I urge you to obey this request.'

'But I love you,' said Psyche, 'and I want to see you. That is natural surely.'

'If you love me,' answered the voice, 'that is enough. I am content that you should love me as your husband. If you saw me, you might adore me, or fear me as a god. It is better that you should be content to love me and be loved by me.'

For a time Psyche was happy. She was content to leave things as her husband had ordered. Each night he came as darkness fell, and before dawn he had fled, leaving her to spend her days peacefully in the palace he had provided for her. But at last she began to think of her absent parents, grieving for her, and of her two sisters, to whom she would have liked to show all the wonders of her home. Beautiful as was this home, it began to seem to her no more than a lovely prison.

One night, when her husband was at her side, she told him of her distress, and at last he promised to let her sisters visit her. This at least would be something to make her feel less a prisoner than before. So Zephyrus, spirit of the west wind, was summoned, and next day he visited the two sisters. He led them by the hands over the mountain and down into Psyche's valley. Psyche greeted them with outstretched arms and took them into her palace. They were shown all the marvels of its golden halls, its marble baths and spacious sleeping chambers; they were attended by the invisible servants and feasted on rare and delicate dishes.

Naturally enough, they became jealous of their sister. They asked her numerous questions. Above all, they wanted to know what her husband was like. She told them that he was a beautiful young man who was at home only in the hours of darkness and spent his days hunting among the hills and vales of the surrounding country.

This answer did not satisfy the sisters, and at last they made her confess that she had never seen him.

On learning this, they began to fill Psyche's mind with doubts and suspicions. They asked her if she had forgotten the words of the oracle of Apollo, that her husband was to be a monster, feared and hated by all men.

'Mark my words,' said one of the sisters, 'he is no fair youth but a serpent who has learned the voice of man to

flatter and cherish you with loving tones, the more easily to strangle and devour you when he has tired of you. No wonder he will not allow himself to be seen by the light of day!'

'I cannot believe it,' protested Psyche.

'Ah, but it is more than likely. Remember, sister, the oracle cannot lie. If you take our advice, you will protect yourself by doing as we say. When your husband is asleep, provide yourself with a lamp and a sharp knife. Take a long look at him, but before he can wake, cut off his head and so rid yourself of the monster. Then once again you will be free. You will be able to enjoy the all pleasures and treasures of your palace without fear of being devoured.'

Psyche indignantly refused to believe her sisters. She told them she would never do as they advised. Yet when they had returned to their own homes, their words remained behind to poison her thoughts. Besides, she was still curious to see her husband.

One day, therefore, overcome by suspicion and curiosity, she hid a lamp and a sharp knife in her room. That night she waited until her husband was sound asleep. Silently the girl uncovered the lamp and held it over the sleeping husband. She was amazed and overcome with joy at what she saw. It was no cruel monster but Eros himself, loveliest of the sons of gods. His manly features were relaxed in sleep, his curled locks strayed over his shoulders, behind which grew his two soft, white-feathered wings – the wings on which he flies here and there upon the earth, causing joy and distress among men and girls as he aims his arrows at their hearts. So this was the monster who had been destined as Psyche's husband. Certainly all men feared and some hated him; certainly he seemed cruel to many. But to Psyche he was her perfect husband and lover.

In her joy and amazement she leaned closer over the

sleeping form of Eros, and burning oil fell from the lamp on to his shoulder. Instantly the god was awakened by the stinging pain of the burns. He saw Psyche with the gleaming knife in her hand. She had forgotten it in the moment of her joy. Without a word Eros rose from the bed, spread his snowy wings and flew from the window. Psyche, with no thought but to follow her husband, leaped through the window after him and fell to the ground. Eros turned in his flight and spoke to her.

'Oh Psyche,' he said, 'how foolish of you to mistrust me and disobey my command. Did I not go against the wishes of my mother by marrying you? Why did you not trust my love? Since you prefer to believe your sisters rather than your lover, you had better go back to them. The only punishment for your disobedience is that I must leave you. Goodbye – love cannot live with suspicion.'

With these bitter words Eros once more spread his wings and flew back to his mother's temple to be healed of the burn on his shoulder. The wretched Psyche was left weeping and lamenting. For hours she cried, until at last she fell asleep from sorrow and exhaustion.

When Psyche awoke, the palace in its stately grove beside the crystal spring had disappeared. She found herself in a field near the city where her sisters lived. She went to them and told them all her misfortunes. They pretended to be sorry, but secretly they rejoiced. Now that the god had left Psyche for ever, might he not take one of them?

So next morning both the sisters rose early without telling anyone and went to the top of the mountain. First one, then the other called upon Zephyrus, spirit of the west wind, to carry her to his lord, the god Eros. Then she leaped into the air, but Zephyrus had not answered their call; so each was dashed to pieces as she fell down the steep slope of the mountain.

Psyche, meanwhile, wandered in every direction in search of her husband. She did not despair of finding him and winning back his love. One day she raised her eyes to the top of a hill on which stood a temple to Demeter, goddess of the harvests. Perhaps she might find her lover there. When she reached the temple, she found that it was filled with the fruits of the harvest – heaps of barley, millet, wheat and maize, all mixed up in a confused mass. Beside them were scattered the tools of the harvesters – rakes, sickles and implements for threshing the grain and binding the sheaves. It was as if the country people, overcome by the heat of the day, had flung everything into the temple, regardless of order. At once, to show her devotion to the gods, Psyche began to sort the grain and arrange the implements of the harvest in proper order. Demeter the goddess, seeing the girl at this pious work, took pity on her.

'Psyche,' said Demeter graciously, 'I am sorry for your distress. I cannot shield you from the anger of Aphrodite, but I can at least give you the best advice to help you in your unhappiness. Go and present yourself to her: ask for her forgiveness and beg her to tell you what you must do to regain her favour. This is the only way in which you may perhaps win back your lost husband.'

Psyche made her way towards the temple of Aphrodite, fearing the angry goddess, yet sure that Demeter was right: to try to please Aphrodite by humble submission and dutiful reverence was the only way by which she might hope for happiness.

Aphrodite was indeed very angry.

'At last,' she cried out when Psyche appeared, her eyes lowered submissively to the ground, 'you realise that you have a mistress. At last you have come to show duty to the goddess to whom you owe reverence. Or have you perhaps come to see your husband, who is still sick of the injury you did him when you dropped burning oil upon him? You have no hope but in showing how dutiful and humble you can be. How otherwise do you suppose a young man like my son can ever again bear to look on a creature so ugly and mis-shapen as you?'

To these insults Psyche made no answer but stood quietly before Aphrodite with her head bowed.

'I will make trial of you,' the goddess went on, 'to see how much patience and skill you are capable of.'

She led the girl to a storehouse at the back of her temple where there was a great heap of grain for her pigeons – wheat, lentils, barley and millet, such as birds love to feed and fatten on. But all the grain was sadly mixed up, just as in the temple of Demeter, only worse.

'You must sort out all this grain by nightfall,' commanded the goddess. 'Put the wheat in one bin, the millet in another, and so on until not one grain is out of place. Do as I command.'

So saying, she left poor Psyche to her impossible task.

Psyche sat weeping before the enormous heap of grain and could do nothing. What was the use of beginning a task so hopeless? But Eros, who knew of her presence in the temple and of her plight, called up the leader of the ants and told her to help Psyche. The ant immediately set out from her home underground and made straight for the store-house. She was followed by a train of other ants in their thousands, and before long they had carried all the grains to their proper bins and performed the task imposed by the cruel goddess.

Aphrodite, meanwhile, was enjoying a splendid banquet of the gods. When it was over, night had fallen. Crowned with roses and perfumed with celestial odours, she went to the storehouse. When she saw that the task had been performed to perfection, she was furious.

'Wicked girl!' she stormed. 'This is not your work. You have been helped by my son. You cannot get my favour by cheating.'

Without another word she flung Psyche a crust of dry bread for her supper and left her to herself.

Next morning the goddess sent for Psyche.

'Today,' she said, 'I have other work for you. Beside the river there is a grove of trees, and under them grazes a flock of sheep. There is no shepherd. The sheep have fleeces of fine golden wool. Fetch me a piece of the wool from every single sheep, and mind, do not miss out one of them. Be off with you!'

Psyche obediently went to the river bank, beyond which stood the grove where grazed the sheep with the golden fleeces. As she was wondering how best to cross the water,

a wind blew through the reeds, which seemed to speak to her with the voice of the river god.

'Dear Psyche,' the voice said, 'do not try to cross the river now and excite the anger of the fierce rams on the other side. They may tear you to pieces with their savage horns, for while the sun is rising towards noon, they are full of rage. But wait until the heat of noon has sent them into the shade. They are calmer then, and you will be able to cross the river in safety and make your way among them unharmed. You will find plenty of their wool sticking to the bushes and brambles in the grove.'

Psyche felt grateful to the kindly river god for his practical advice, which she began to follow as soon as the afternoon sun had driven the sheep and the fierce rams into the quiet shade. Going swiftly from bush to bush, she collected a

huge armful of the golden fleeces and took them back to Aphrodite. The goddess received them with an ill grace.

'You could not have done this without help from another,' she said sourly. 'I am still not persuaded that you ever manage to do anything useful by your own efforts. I have yet another task for you. Here, take this box and go with it down to the underworld. Present yourself at the temple of the queen, Persephone. Ask for her to put a little of her beauty into the box, that I may wear it tonight at the banquet of the gods. In looking after my sick son, wounded by your foolishness, I have lost a little of my own beauty and must repair it. Go at once, and do not be long.'

Left to herself with the box, Psyche now believed that her end had come. How could she, a mere unprotected mortal, go alone to the dread kingdom of Hades, the gloomy shades where all men fear to tread? So in order to bring upon herself the end which she felt to be near and get to the under-world by the quickest possible way, she climbed a hill on which stood a high tower. From this she prepared to throw herself to destruction. But the voice of an unseen presence called to her from the tower.

'Fair Psyche, why do you despair? Have you lost the courage that carried you through all previous trials? Is this the way to reach the underworld and fetch back what you have been told to fetch? No. There is a better way. I shall lead you to the entrance of a cave, through which you shall pass in safety to the kingdom of the dead. You shall pass unharmed the dreaded Cerberus, the three-headed monster who guards the entrance. Charon the ferryman shall row you in safety across the River Styx. Come, take my hand, and you shall have courage to face the ordeal that lies before you.'

Then the unseen presence led Psyche to the entrance of the cave and bade her farewell.

'One thing I must warn you against,' said the voice. 'When you have got what you need, do not once open the box and look into it. It is not for a mortal woman to pry into the secrets of divine beauty.'

Psyche did as she was told, obeying her adviser in every detail until she had returned safely from the dreaded journey.

She presented herself at the throne of Persephone and made known the wishes of Aphrodite. The queen of the underworld gave her what she requested, and Psyche returned by the way she had come, filled with joy and thanksgiving to see once more the light of the sun. She began to travel swiftly back towards her mistress Aphrodite, but curiosity seized her. She was suddenly overcome by an irresistible desire to see what was in the box. Perhaps a little of Persephone's beauty might alight on her own faded cheeks and make her more desirable than ever in the eyes of her husband, if ever she should see him again. Swiftly she unclasped the lid of the box and opened it. In it she saw nothing. Nothing whatever was visible, and the box seemed full only of the intense darkness of death. From this arose the vapours of a profound sleep, which swirled about Psyche's head. Within a few instants she had fainted away and lay like one dead beside the road.

Eros meanwhile had recovered from his burn and was eager to see his beloved wife once more. He had forgiven her for her disobedience. He slipped through the open window of his room and flew by instinct to the place where Psyche lay. He knew at once what had happened. With his magic powers he gathered up the sleep from Psyche's body, replaced it in the box and closed the lid. Then he touched her with an arrow and she awoke.

'Oh faithless Psyche,' said Eros, 'once more you have almost died through that same curiosity which made you

break your promise to me. But you are safe. Go now to my
mother and give her the box. Make haste, for she is waiting
impatiently.'

As soon as Psyche had taken up the box and begun to
make her way towards Aphrodite's temple, Eros rose swiftly
into the air and presented himself at the throne of Zeus,

chief of all the gods, on Mount Olympus. Zeus was awaiting the nightly banquet of the immortals, which was soon to begin. Eros pleaded with him for the life of his beloved and for the favour of Aphrodite, whom Psyche had offended unintentionally. Zeus was moved by the young man's entreaties. He sent his messenger Hermes of the winged feet to fetch Psyche up to the divine assembly. When Psyche appeared before him, Zeus greeted her and offered her a cup of nectar, the wine of the gods.

'Drink this, Psyche,' he said kindly, 'and be one of us – be immortal, even as a goddess.'

Then Zeus commanded that there should be a feast in honour of the marriage of Eros and Psyche, who were to remain united for ever. Thus, after many trials, the two lovers were joined in perpetual happiness in the company of the gods. Even proud Aphrodite forgave Psyche when she saw that her dear son Eros could not be happy without her.

Ceyx and Alcyone

Ceyx was King of Thessaly, where he ruled justly and peaceably. He was a handsome man and the son of Hesperus, the evening star. His dutiful and loving wife was Alcyone, daughter of Aeolus, in whose keeping are all the winds of heaven. Ceyx was in mourning for the death of his brother. At this event strange and terrible prodigies had occurred, and this made Ceyx afraid of what might come. He decided, therefore, to journey to Caros in Ionia, to consult the oracle of Apollo. When he told his wife Alcyone about this, she shuddered and turned pale.

'What is wrong?' asked Ceyx.

'Have I offended you, that you must leave me?' asked Alcyone. 'Do not make this voyage. It is dangerous to venture out to sea. Believe me, I know the winds, and they will do their worst to engulf you in storms and wreck your ship.'

Ceyx told her he must go.

'Well then,' said Alcyone, 'take me with you so that I may share your perils. Don't leave me at home to imagine your dangers and hardships.'

Ceyx would have liked to grant her wish, but he could not bear to expose her to the dangers of the sea. So he told

24

her he must depart as soon as the wind permitted, and said farewell.

'I swear to you,' he said at parting, 'by my father Hesperus, the evening star, whom I call upon for his protection, that I will return to you before two full moons have shown themselves in the sky.'

With tears and vain entreaties Alcyone watched her husband as he stood on the deck of the ship, which slowly disappeared from view. Then she returned home, her heart full of foreboding, and threw herself on her bed in terror and despair. She feared she had seen the last of her beloved Ceyx.

Alcyone's fears were all too well founded. For when little more than half King Ceyx's course had been travelled, the winds arose, the waves swelled and whitened to angry foam and, as night came on, a storm burst over the ship. In vain

did the sailors haul on their ropes and draw in the sails. In vain did they ship their oars and lash them to the sides of the vessel. Night fell swiftly, lit only by forked lightning and made terrible by the screeching of the wind and the crashing of thunder. Rain fell in torrents as if to make the whole world one mass of seething water.

Courage sank and hope failed. Death seemed certain. The sailors in despair thought of their homes and the loved ones they would see no more. Ceyx thought only of his wife Alcyone, whose name was ever on his lips, as if she were a goddess to whom he was praying. He longed for her comforting arms but rejoiced that she was safe at home in Thessaly.

Then the whole world seemed to explode in one tremendous crash. The mast broke in half and the rudder was torn from the ship's stern. Some of the sailors were swept off the decks, to sink in the boiling waves and rise no more. Others clutched at fragments of wreckage. Ceyx clung to a plank and shouted for help. His cries were in vain. With Alcyone's name upon his lips he was dashed from the plank by a wave as high as a palace. As he sank, he prayed that his body might be washed ashore at the feet of his wife. At least he would be mourned and buried by her he loved.

Alcyone, meanwhile, knew nothing of all this. She counted the days until her husband's return, busying herself in getting ready the palace and preparing the garments she would wear on the day of thanksgiving. She prayed incessantly to the gods for his safety, and especially to Hera, wife of Zeus, king of all the gods.

Gods alone are all-knowing, and Hera knew that Ceyx, for whom Alcyone prayed, was already dead. She could not bear to hear the vain prayers and entreaties of the Queen. Somehow she must be told of her husband's sad fate. So the goddess summoned her messenger, Iris, and sent her on an errand to the cave of the god of sleep. Iris, whom mortals see as the rainbow, put on her robe of many colours and sped across the sky. The cave of sleep was a dark and drowsy den, whence flowed Lethe, river of forgetfulness. On a black couch, draped in a cloak of sable, slept the god. Iris woke him up and said:

'I come from the goddess Hera. She commands you to send to Alcyone, Queen of Thessaly, a dream in which she will learn how Ceyx, her husband, was lately drowned in a storm at sea.'

The god called up Morpheus, one of his sons, and bade him go and present himself, in the form of the drowned Ceyx, at the bed of Alcyone, as she slept. When he had done this, Iris sped away and the god of sleep yawned and closed his eyes.

Morpheus, who has the power to assume the shapes and voices of men, flew noiselessly to the palace of Alcyone. There he laid aside his dusky wings and took on the shape of a drowned man, his hair and beard coated with salt, his limbs entwined with seaweed. Then he stood in the pale half-light of early dawn at the foot of Alcyone's bed.

'Do you recognise your husband Ceyx?' he asked, tears streaming from his salt-reddened eyes. He spoke with the voice of the drowned king. 'I am the spirit of your husband, lost in the stormy sea. Pray no more for my return, but give me your tears and lamentations, so that I may go to the underworld mourned by her I never ceased to love and to call upon even as the waves filled my mouth.'

Alcyone, on hearing these words, groaned in her sleep and stretched forth her hands to embrace her husband's ghost. But Morpheus vanished and, as Alcyone awoke, she knew that her dream had been a vision of the truth.

'My fears did not deceive me,' she cried in her agony. 'Now I know the cruel waves have devoured him. He should have taken me with him, so that in death we would not have been divided. I cannot live without him. I must go and share his death.'

It was now dawn. Quickly the Queen arose and prepared for her last journey. She hastened down to the seashore and found the spot near the harbour where she had last seen her husband. There, not two months ago, she had gazed out to sea and watched the sails of his ship disappearing over the horizon, bearing the man she loved to his destruction. Then, as she looked out across the water, she saw something floating gently towards the land. The waves, now peaceful, carried it steadily nearer. At last Alcyone could see that it was the body of a drowned man. She trembled and clasped her hands together in torment as she recognised the body as that of Ceyx. She stretched out her arms towards it and cried:

'Is this your promised return, my loved one? Is it thus that you come back to me over the pitiless ocean?'

A mole or breakwater had been built out into the sea to protect the harbour from the force of the waves. From this Alcyone could get nearer to the floating form of Ceyx. Without a moment's hesitation she ran to the end of the mole and leaped into the water to join her husband, from whom she could not bear to be parted. But at the instant of her leap she was changed into a bird and flew skimming across the water. From her throat, in the voice of a bird, came a song of deepest lamentation. She alighted on the waves beside the pale body of her husband, enfolding it in her wings. With her horny beak she strove to kiss the lifeless body. At this Ceyx too was changed into a living bird. The faithful pair were thus reunited as a reward by the gods for their devotion to each other. They mated and had their brood of young ones every year.

So was born the race of the kingfisher, known to the

28

Greeks by the name of Alcyone or, as we call it, the Halcyon. Each winter, for seven calm days, Alcyone broods over her nest, which floats peacefully upon the waters. By this mariners may know that the sea is safe to voyage over, and Aeolus, father of Alcyone, controls the winds and will not let them arise to drive the storm clouds across the sea. In these few halcyon days the sea is the playground of Aeolus' grandchildren, the little kingfishers.

Orpheus and Eurydice

Apollo, god of the Sun and greatest of all musicians, had a son by the Muse Calliope. The Muses were nine goddesses who lived on Mount Helicon and inspired poets, writers and musicians. The son of Apollo and Calliope was called Orpheus.

As might be expected of the son of such gifted parents, Orpheus proved to have a more than ordinary talent for music. His father gave him a lyre of great beauty, cunningly fashioned so that the music of its seven strings was of unusual power and sweetness. But greater than the sweetness of the lyre was the skill of its owner. As the young man, dark-haired and with shining eyes, went about the countryside singing to the strains of his lyre, not only did men and women marvel to hear him; even mountains seemed to be raising their heads in wonder. The streams stayed their rushing to listen to him, and even the very rocks lost some of their hardness at the sound of his music. He became familiar among the woods and mountains of Thrace, which were inhabited by wild animals. But Orpheus went in no fear of even the fiercest creature; for such was the power of his music that the very wolves and lions would lie down at his feet and draw in their claws, lulled to gentleness as the young man's fingers moved over the strings of his lyre. The harmless creatures, the fawn and the antelope, would stretch themselves out beside the lion, sensing that even the king of beasts would not harm them so long as Orpheus played and sang. The trees crowded together about the musician, giving shade to him and his audience; the winds were still, and in the branches sat the dove and the eagle, side by side. Never before had such music charmed the ear of man and beast alike.

In Thrace lived the nymphs of stream and woodland, and they too came to listen to Orpheus. The wood nymphs were called Dryads, and among them the most beautiful was Eurydice. No sooner did she cast eyes on the young musician than she fell in love with him. Raising his head from the lyre, Orpheus as quickly fell in love with the Dryad, and resolved to marry her. Their courting was not long, and soon

they had agreed to become man and wife. But at the wedding ceremony Fate was not on their side. For when Hymen, the god of marriage, held aloft the lighted torch, it burned, not with a clear golden flame, but with black smoke which drifted over the assembly in a thick and ominous cloud. So the eyes of the crowd, instead of being filled with joy, smarted with tears of pain. In vain did Orpheus play his best; in vain the nymphs prayed to the gods to send better omens.

Not long afterwards Eurydice and the other Dryads were wandering through the woods when a young man named Aristaeus caught sight of her and determined to win her for himself. He tried to seize her, but she fled from him through the trees, and he pursued her. In her flight Eurydice chanced to step on a snake in the grass. It bit her foot, and she died of the poison. Aristaeus, her pursuer, was a shepherd and a bee-keeper, and after the death of Eurydice the nymphs, her companions, poisoned his bees in revenge, so that they died.

So great was the shock to Orpheus that he could not believe Eurydice was really dead. Might not his music, that had moved even stones, soften the hearts of the gods? For they were all-powerful and could give him back his wife if they wished. So Orpheus played upon his lyre more ravishingly than ever, raising his voice in sorrowful lamentation. The gods of the earth were moved, but they could do nothing for him, since the dead do not stay upon the earth but descend into the realm of the stern god Hades and his queen, Persephone. Here in the timeless shades the spirits of the dead wander aimlessly, and never look again upon the green fields and woods of the upper world.

In despair Orpheus went to seek his lost wife in the regions of the dead. He went down into the underworld by a steep and narrow way which began in a gloomy cave. Down and down the path wound until it reached the grey and dreary realm of Hades. Passing through crowds of ghosts, Orpheus made his way towards the throne of the king and queen. At the sight of the wild-eyed musician with his lyre, the god Hades raised his hand for silence and bade the stranger play. With his right hand Orpheus struck the lyre and, lifting his voice, began to plead and mourn in tones which moved the hardest hearts and brought tears to the eyes of many.

'O god and goddess,' sang Orpheus, 'to whom we must all come at last, listen, I pray, to my tale, for I speak the truth. Perhaps you ask why I, a living man, have come of my own free will to your kingdom. I am not here to spy out the secrets of Hades nor to fight against the monster who guards your gates. I am come to plead for your mercy and to beg you to give back life to my beloved Eurydice, who was slain by the cruel viper when our wedding rites were scarcely over. Give her back to me, I beg, for she has done no harm and broken no vow. Gods of the underworld, we shall all come under your rule in time. When our time has come, we shall give thanks to the gods for our love and our lives, but until she has lived her proper span, give her back to me, I implore you.'

So piteously did Orpheus lament, with such skill did he draw harmony from the strings that the inhabitants of Hades came from near and far to hear his music. The ghosts came in crowds, like flocks of birds coming home to roost at dusk, or like showers of dead leaves driven by the autumn wind. There were boys and men, unmarried girls, the spirits of great heroes and of nameless ones who had died in battle on land or sea. All who heard were touched to the heart by the music of Orpheus; all pitied the young man whose loss had inspired him to songs never heard before on earth or in the underworld.

Among those who heard Orpheus were the prisoners in Hades, doomed to suffer eternal punishment for their crimes on earth. Tantalus was one. He was condemned to lie beneath a tree at the edge of a pool. Every time he stretched out his hand to gather fruit, a wind blew the branches out of reach. Every time he approached the pool to quench his thirst, the water drew back. Another was Ixion, whose punishment was to be tied to a wheel which turned for ever. When Orpheus sang, the wheel stood still, and Ixion was for a while relieved of his torment. Sisyphus, for his crimes on earth, was condemned to roll a heavy stone up a hill; as soon as it reached the top, it rolled down again, so that his labour was eternal. For the first time he was allowed to rest upon his stone half-way up the hill, while Orpheus lamented. For the first time, too, the cheeks of the Furies were wet with tears. These were among the most terrible deities in Hades – three winged women whose purpose was to avenge crimes against family ties, such as the killing of a parent or a child. Some say that their look was made fiercer by writhing serpents which crowned their heads, like the serpents of the gorgon Medusa. Now even the snakes ceased their writhing and hissing to listen to Orpheus.

By the time the song was finished, Persephone, queen of the underworld, could not restrain her pity, and with tear-filled eyes she looked at her husband and pleaded for the life of Eurydice. Hades, stern king, consented, and the young bride was summoned from among the newly arrived ghosts. Limping upon her wounded foot, Eurydice appeared, pale and beautiful, before the throne. Long and lovingly Orpheus looked at her, but he dared not approach until the king had given his judgement. Because of his steadfastness in love, said the king, Orpheus would be allowed to take her back to the earth on one condition: he was to lead the way, and Eurydice would follow. He must not look back at her, even for an instant, until they reached the upper air. If he did, he would lose her once more – this time for ever.

34

Eagerly Orpheus embraced his wife. Then, taking leave of the king and queen, they began the journey back to earth. Orpheus went in front, Eurydice behind, as they had been bidden. Once the gloomy regions of ghosts were passed, they came to a place of terrible darkness and silence, groping their way between rocks and through dark passages where icy water dripped about them, and jagged rocks tore their clothes. Then they began to climb, up and up along the winding track by which Orpheus had come. Panting, he reached a sort of ledge or platform not far from where the track led into the cave where it would end in the light of day. Suddenly a madness overcame Orpheus. A terrible fear for his loved Eurydice made him forget his promise to the king of the underworld. He looked back to see if he could make out her form in the darkness behind him, and in that instant she was lost to him.

A great roll of thunder came from the underworld

beneath, as if the Furies were expressing their wrath at Orpheus's forgetfulness. There is no forgiveness in Hades. Amidst the thunder Orpheus heard the voice of Eurydice:

'O Orpheus, the Fates are calling me back. Unseen hands are dragging me down. I feel faint, and I no longer have any power to resist.'

In vain did Orpheus stretch out his arms to embrace her. She floated like a cloud of grey smoke back into the depths of Hades. He had lost her for ever.

For seven months Orpheus wandered amidst the desolate rocks and mountains of Thrace, lamenting the second death of Eurydice in strains which softened the stones about him and melted the hard hearts of wolves and lions. But his song had no power to pierce the ears of the guardians of the underworld, and he called down bitter curses upon their heads.

'O gloomy powers,' he sang, 'O savage Furies, let an everlasting curse fall upon your flinty hearts. Wolves are not too cruel to be moved; granite cliffs are softened by my grief. You alone remain immovable in your unjust and hellish fury against one whose only fault was to love too much the wife you have taken from him.'

The story of Orpheus's death is as sad as that of Eurydice's, and more terrible. The Thracian nymphs, Eurydice's former companions, tried to console Orpheus, but he would not listen to them. He wished only to be left to mourn for his wife alone. But they pursued him with sweet songs and wooed him with garlands of flowers.

'Eurydice is dead,' they said. 'She will never return again. Take another wife. Take one of us, and she will make you happier than ever you were before.'

Still Orpheus would not listen, and in the end the nymphs' love was turned to hate. They now wished only to destroy Orpheus.

One day they were celebrating the festival of the god
Dionysus. The music and dancing maddened them, and one
of them, seeing Orpheus a long way off, cried:

'See, there is the man who scorns us, the man who despises
our kindness and love. He no longer deserves to live!'

Swiftly she ran, spear in hand, to where Orpheus was
playing a sad lament on his lyre. When she was within range,
she hurled the spear. But the spear was turned away from
Orpheus by the power of his music. So also were the stones
which other maidens threw at the young man. At this the
enraged nymphs lifted their voices in a scream of anger,
which utterly drowned the notes of the lyre. Orpheus's music
had no longer any power to protect him, and in a moment
a spear struck him in the breast and he was killed. Then the
shrieking nymphs tore his body limb from limb and flung
the remains far and wide. They cut off his head, and threw

37

it, together with the lyre, into the River Hebrus. Such was the revenge of Eurydice's former companions on her unhappy husband. Such was his reward for loving her too dearly.

The head of Orpheus floated slowly down the river, the lyre beside it. His eyes were closed and his black hair, stained with blood, streamed behind him. From his open mouth came a long last lament; and magical notes sounded from the floating lyre, so that the trees along the river bank bowed their heads in sympathy, and the shores echoed with the dead man's sorrow. At last the head of Orpheus reached the island of Lesbos, where it was buried. The lyre was taken up by the gods and given a place among the stars in heaven. Orpheus's mother, Calliope, and her sister Muses gathered up the torn limbs and buried them in a grove in Libethra. Here, it is said, the nightingales sing over the grave of Orpheus with a more piercing sweetness than in any other part of Greece.

The spirit of Orpheus went down to the underworld, where once the living man had been. Eagerly he sought the spirit of his dead Eurydice, and together they wander through the grey wastes of Hades, happy in each other's company, happy in the knowledge that never again can they be divided.

Theseus

1 The Journey to Athens

Queen Aethra lived in Troizen with her little son Theseus. His father Aegeus had left Troizen to become king of Athens. Before he left, he had raised a great stone and laid under it a pair of enchanted sandals and a curved sword in a sheath of ivory. He told Aethra that as soon as their son was strong enough to raise the stone, he was to take the sword and the sandals and make his way to Athens, where he would reign as king after his father.

Golden-haired Theseus grew straight and strong, learning to run and wrestle like the other boys of Troizen. Soon he became their leader, for he was a more powerful wrestler than they, and a faster runner. He could leap further and higher than all the others, and throw the javelin straighter. He was, too, a fine hunter, taking great delight in pursuing the leopard and the antelope through the vales and hills that lay about his home. Everyone acknowledged the strength, the courage and the manly grace of the young prince.

More than once the boy looked at the great stone which, as his mother had told him, hid the gifts left by his father. As little boys, he and his companions had often made pretence of raising it to see what was underneath, but many years were to pass before even Theseus, the strongest of them, was able to lift it so much as an inch from the ground. How Theseus longed to claim possession of his birthright and go in search of adventure, as the hero Heracles had done before him.

At last the day came, as Aethra knew it must. One fine spring morning the young man, for such he now was, bestrode the great stone, bent over it, placed the fingers of both hands beneath the farther edge and heaved with all his might. Almost before he knew he had succeeded, he felt the stone yield to his strength. Leaping aside, he was in time to avoid it as it toppled over backwards, revealing a cavity underneath. In it were the bright sword in its ivory scabbard and the enchanted sandals, just as his father had left them all those years before.

'Now,' said Theseus to his mother, 'I have won my birthright, and I must set out at once to greet my father in Athens, just as you have always said I should.'

Half in tears and half in joy, Aethra gave orders that a sacrifice should be made at the temple, in order that her son should have protection when he set out on the morrow. The wise men of Troizen counselled the youth to set sail and cross the gulf which divided their land from Athens. But Theseus had other plans. The country between was infested with brigands and monsters, who harassed and terrorized the people. Simply to take the short way by sea would be to avoid all these dangers and lose the chance to prove himself a hero. So Theseus determined to go the long way round by land. Heracles, his hero, would have done the same. The youth could then prove his strength and courage, and show himself fit to reign in Athens when the time came. In vain did the elders plead with him to take the easier way.

So next morning, as the sun rose over the eastern hills, the golden-haired youth made his sacrifice to the gods, embraced his mother, and bade farewell to the companions of his boyhood. All cheered and wished him luck as he strode out to seek his fame and fortune. The sword was buckled securely by his side and the enchanted sandals bore him swiftly on his way. It was not long before he met his first adventure.

At Epidaurus, not far along the road, the ground was strewn with human bones, the grisly remains of the victims of the giant Periphetes, known to all the countryside as the Club-bearer. With a roar the giant plunged from a thicket and bore straight down upon the young man, brandishing above his shoulders the great bronze club which was the terror of all who came that way. The giant commanded

Theseus to go no further, but Theseus, stepping nimbly aside as the monstrous weapon came crashing down, turned swiftly and struck Periphetes with his sword. For a while the two fought desperately, filling the air with their heavy breathing and with cries of pain or triumph. At length the youth and nimbleness of the young man began to tell. Periphetes's breath came more heavily, and the terrible blows of his club fell more slowly about the young man's body. He began to fear that at last he had met his match. Already wounded more than once, he suddenly fell to the ground as Theseus aimed a deadly stroke at his heart. The fight was over. The giant lay dead on the ground, and the bronze club rolled from his grasp. Triumphantly Theseus replaced his sword in the sheath at his side and picked up the club. This, he was determined, was his weapon by right, and for the rest of his journey he carried it with him. Heavy as it was, he could wield it with scarcely an effort.

The shepherds and shepherdesses of the region came to pay homage to the young hero and thank him for their deliverance from the dreaded Club-bearer. Then, as they cheered him on his way, they warned him of the next danger he would meet further along the road to Athens. This was a cruel man named Sinis, known as the Pine-bender. The reason for his nickname was this: it was his delight to seize an unlucky traveller and bind him fast with ropes. Then, such was his mighty strength, he would bend two young pines to the ground until they almost touched each other, and tie his victim partly to one tree, partly to the other. Then he would let them go, and the miserable traveller would be torn in half and his limbs flung far and wide, to be devoured by vultures. Part might hang from the tops of the trees, a ghastly warning to others.

With stern and resolute features Theseus strode towards

the haunt of the Pine-bender. It was not long before he encountered him. The man rudely ordered the young wayfarer to stop and give himself up. For answer Theseus ran towards him, flourishing the bronze club he had taken from Periphetes.

'This weapon I took from the giant Periphetes!' he cried. 'As I served him, so shall I serve all tyrants!'

So great was the surprise of Sinis at Theseus's defiance that he had no time to step aside as the bronze club was swung through the air. Felled to the ground, he screamed for mercy, but Theseus swiftly bound him with ropes and tied him to two of the trees in the grove where he had for so long spread terror. When Theseus let go of the saplings, the Pine-bender himself was torn asunder and his remains fed the crows for miles around. So ended yet another monster in human shape, and the neighbourhood was made safe for travellers.

The next episode in Theseus's progress to Athens took place near the town of Crommyon. Here he heard reports of yet another enemy to peaceful people – not a tyrant or a giant this time but a monstrous wild sow. This ferocious animal lurked in the woods about the town, preying on sheep and young pigs, frightening the farmers and even attacking young children, who ran screaming to their parents if they so much as caught sight of the beast. At once Theseus strode off into the woods where it had last been reported. He had not gone far before he heard the crackling of dry leaves and undergrowth. Then in a clearing he caught sight of the sow. It was of enormous size and covered all over with spiky bristles. Its short, powerful legs dug into the ground as it rushed towards the young man, snorting with savage fury. As he prepared to swing his bronze club, Theseus had just time to catch sight of the animal's sharp pointed teeth and its wicked little red eyes, set close to its snout. One blow of the great club was sufficient to knock the monster senseless. Then he cut off its head and bore it in triumph back to Crommyon, where his victory was celebrated with feasts and dancing. The countryside was rid for ever of one more danger.

As Theseus went on, his feet made lighter by the enchanted sandals, the road became steeper and rougher. Presently it was no more than a narrow track between the hills and the sea. A passing stranger warned him of the presence of the bandit Sciron, who haunted the craggy cliff that bore his name. It was the bandit's practice, the stranger told Theseus, to make everyone who came that way kneel down and wash his feet. Then he would seize the man while he knelt and pitch him headlong over the cliff into the sea far below. Here lurked a great tortoise, who waited to devour Sciron's victims. Thus, said the stranger, cautious wayfarers like himself were obliged to go inland and take a longer way round in order to avoid the bandit.

Theseus thanked the stranger for his warning – but nothing would turn him from his course. Up the steep path he went until he came to the summit of Sciron's cliff. Everything turned out just as he had been told. Astride the narrow path stood Sciron, an uncouth and brawny ruffian, his face scarcely visible through the shaggy locks that hung down about it.

'Young man!' roared Sciron as soon as Theseus came into view. 'You shall not pass this way before doing as I order you. I demand of all comers that they kneel down at my feet and wash them, for I am lord of this land.'

Instantly the young man obeyed, going down on one knee before the bandit. Taking a filthy rag that Sciron gave him, he prepared to wash his feet.

'Place your right foot on my knee, Master,' he said cunningly, 'so that I may do your bidding.'

As soon as Sciron's foot was firmly on his knee, Theseus sprang up, seized the bandit by the wrist and twisted him over his shoulder before he knew what was happening. It was a trick that he had learnt when wrestling as a boy in Troizen. With a roar of surprise and anger, Sciron attempted to escape from Theseus's grasp. But the young man was too quick for him. The bandit was hurled over the edge of the cliff, his arms and legs whirling in all directions. Nothing could save him, though what became of him is not certain. Some say he was devoured by the very tortoise to which he had fed so many hapless victims. Others say that he escaped the tortoise but was turned into a rock which can be seen to this very day under the cliff that bears his name.

Another evil-doer whom Theseus encountered as he drew nearer to Athens was a man named Procrustes or the Stretcher. He had a particularly cruel way of dealing with his victims. If he saw a harmless traveller who looked as if he was tired, he would invite him with a show of courtesy to accept the hospitality of his cottage. In it he had a bedstead on which he invited his guest to lie down. But he insisted that the traveller should fit the bed exactly. If he was too short, Procrustes stretched his limbs until they were long enough. Thus the bedstead was really an instrument of torture. If the unfortunate guest was too long, however, Procrustes lopped off enough of his legs to make him fit. When Theseus reached the cottage of this horrible butcher, he was invited inside, as other travellers were.

'You look tired,' said Procrustes. 'Won't you lie down on the bed I keep for my guests?'

Theseus made as if to do so; then, as Procrustes prepared to tie him down, he jumped up and seized his attacker by the throat. A wrestling match followed. Both men fought with furious determination, but the young man was more than a match for Procrustes. When the torturer was tied safely to his own bedstead and could struggle no more, Theseus said:

'As my enemies use other men, so they are used by me!'

Although Procrustes exactly fitted the bedstead, Theseus ended his life by cutting off his head. In this way he freed the country for ever from one more evil brigand.

Thus the young hero overcame all the dangers of the journey, but his greatest danger lay ahead. It awaited him in Athens itself, where his father Aegeus reigned with the sorceress Medea, who had been the wife of Jason, as his queen. It must be remembered that Aegeus had never seen Theseus since he was a baby, so that he had no idea that the unknown young hero who strode into Athens in triumph was his own son. But Medea knew by means of witchcraft, and she wanted the throne of Athens for her own son. She feared that Theseus, being the king's eldest child, would take the throne and the kingdom for himself. This she determined to prevent at all costs. She murmured in the king's ear that the young stranger was coming to plot against him and raise a rebellion.

'I know this, by magic arts,' she told Aegeus. 'Your only hope is to rid the kingdom of him before he wins the hearts of the people and makes himself popular. He is even now on his way to the palace. I have prepared a draught of wine and have put into it a few drops of poison which I myself have distilled from herbs. He will die instantly.'

Aegeus was a weak man and agreed to allow his queen to kill the young man in this way.

Amidst the applause of some citizens of Athens who had already heard of Theseus's brave exploits, the hero walked swiftly and gracefully down the great hall to where Aegeus sat on his royal throne. The king rose and greeted him. Then he held out the cup of wine which Medea had prepared. Theseus was about to raise it to his lips when suddenly his father noticed the carved ivory scabbard of the sword which he himself had left long ago under the stone in far-off Troizen.

'My son, my son!' he cried. 'Do not drink! The wine is poisoned.'

As he spoke, he dashed the cup from Theseus's hand, and the wine spilled harmlessly on the floor. There was a moment of astonished silence. Then Aegeus ordered the palace guards to seize Medea. But she had already fled from the hall. The instant she saw that Aegeus recognised Theseus, she knew that her plot had failed. Before anyone knew what had become of her, she had leapt into her winged chariot and was borne high in the air by enchantment. She did not stop till she had travelled far east into Asia and was never more seen in Greece.

Meanwhile Theseus had recovered from his amazement.

He eagerly admitted that he was the son of Aethra and had taken the sword from under the stone, as had been ordained. Aegeus embraced his son and ordered a great feast to celebrate the coming of the young hero. Golden-haired Theseus glowed with triumph as he told the story of his adventures on the road to Athens. Garlanded by a cheering throng, he displayed the sword and its carved ivory sheath and the terrible bronze weapon he had won from the dreaded Clubbearer when first he began his journey. So Theseus remained many days in Athens, sharing his glory with the father he had so long desired to see.

2 The Minotaur

For a long time Theseus continued to live in Athens at his father's palace. He was honoured by all the people for his brave deeds, and he continued to fight against the enemies of Athens, winning for himself new renown every day. Then came the spring, and with it sadness fell upon the city.

The reason for it was this. Far to the south in an island named Crete lived King Minos, the ruler of the sea. He had had a son who had journeyed to Athens some years before to take part in the games. He was a splendid wrestler and runner, and King Aegeus had become jealous of his success. So he had the son of Minos murdered. This was a shameful deed, and Minos was quick to take revenge. He sent warships to make battle against the Athenians, and such damage did he do, that Aegeus was forced to beg for peace. Minos made peace on one condition – and very harsh and grievous it was. Each spring seven young men and seven girls were to be sent to Crete as food for the monster called the Minotaur. This creature had the head and horns of a bull and the body of a man. It was kept in a maze or labyrinth which had been cunningly constructed by the great craftsman Daedalus so that once inside it, it was almost impossible to find the way out. The Minotaur's food was human flesh, and Minos was obliged to feed it on living people.

So every spring the Athenians were forced to choose seven youths and seven girls by lot, and they were sent in a ship with black sails as tribute to King Minos. Great was the sorrow that fell upon the people of Athens: and spring, which should have been a season of rejoicing, was a season

of mourning. Instead of feasts and dancing they went about weeping and sorrowing, as one by one their children or their brothers and sisters were chosen to be food of the monster.

As soon as he knew of this yearly sacrifice, Theseus determined to put an end to it. When lots were being drawn as to which of the wretched youths of Athens were to be sacrificed, he spoke to his father.

'Father,' he said, 'I will myself go with the ship to Crete. Either I shall slay this terrible creature, this bull-headed man, or I shall be killed.'

'No, my son,' cried Aegeus. 'You must not go. The lot has not fallen on you, and I cannot allow it. You are to be king of Athens when I die. That is your fate, not death in the labyrinth in Crete.'

'If other young men of Athens go,' argued Theseus, 'why should not I? Let me take the same chance with the others.

Am I not slayer of the giant Periphetes, the pine-bender Sinis, and the villain Procrustes? I am not frightened of the Minotaur. I shall go with the others.'

Aegeus was obliged to give in. With a heavy heart he saw his son join the six other young men and the seven girls, and go aboard the ship with the black sails. It was arranged that, when the ship returned to Athens, the sails should be changed for white ones if the voyage had been successful. If not – if Theseus was slain by the Cretan monster – the sails were to remain black.

All the citizens of Athens were gathered by the quay, as slowly the sails were hoisted and the ship began to move away to the south. Bitter tears were shed by the mothers and fathers, the brothers and sisters, of those in the ship. But with a high heart golden-haired Theseus stood at the stern of the ship and waved farewell to his grieving yet proud father. Sacrifices were offered to the gods and prayers were said in the temples, begging for the safe return of the expedition.

All too quickly the voyage was over. The servants and soldiers of King Minos were awaiting the arrival of the Athenians in Crete to escort the unwilling party to the palace of the King. The palace and grounds were of the utmost magnificence and splendour, but the luckless youths and maidens had no eyes for its beauty. Nevertheless, Minos received them courteously and asked them to partake of a banquet in their honour. They were to stay overnight at his palace, and in the morning they would be driven through the great bronze gate of the labyrinth as food for the monstrous Minotaur.

At the banquet Ariadne, the daughter of the king, could not take her eyes off the handsome stranger who was the leader of the party. She fell in love with Theseus at first sight and determined to save him if she could. After the banquet she walked with him in the palace grounds, and as they walked she said:

'Handsome Athenian, I am grieved that you and your companions must be sacrificed tomorrow. It is a terrible thing.'

'Then ask your father to spare us,' said Theseus.

'He will not listen to me. He is stern and revengeful. Every year it has been my unhappy lot to see your young men and maidens go away to be slain by the Minotaur. My father will only say that the monster, which is sacred, must have human victims.'

'Then how can you help us?'

'If I can find a way of helping you, you must take me back to Athens with you, for there will be no safety for me in Crete if it is found out that I have helped you.'

'Very well. You shall come with us. But how are we to bring this about?'

Cautiously Ariadne drew a sword from under her cloak and gave it to Theseus.

'It is enchanted,' she told him. 'No creature can withstand this sword.'

Then she handed to him a ball of woollen thread.

'Take this too' she said. 'You will need it.'

'What for?' asked Theseus.

'Once you have slain the Minotaur, you must find your way out of the maze. When you get in, tie one end of the wool to the doorpost and let the ball unroll as you go. You have only to follow the wool back and you will find your way out.'

Theseus listened carefully to these instructions, and early in the morning the young men and maidens were led to the entrance of the maze. Their guards opened the great bronze door and drove them in. As soon as the door was locked behind them, Theseus bade his companions remain hidden close to the beginning of the maze. They wished him good fortune as he fastened the end of the woollen ball to the doorpost and made his way forward, gripping firmly in his right hand the sword which Ariadne had given him. Through the cunning labyrinth he stole, this way and that, listening intently for any sound the hidden monster might make. As he went, the ball of wool gradually unwound, until very little of it was left in the pocket of his tunic. Suddenly he heard the sound of snorting and the scuffling of some clumsy body. He judged that the Minotaur must be round the next corner of the passage he was exploring. Almost before he knew it, the creature was in front of him, scarcely a stone's throw away. He saw the great black head, the cruel horns, the wicked eyes, and even Theseus's heart began to thump. Nevertheless, he tightened his grip on the sword and awaited the charge that must surely come. Sure enough, the Minotaur lowered its head, gave a terrifying bellow and rushed towards Theseus. Nimbly the young man jumped to one side, and as the monster passed him, he aimed a sword thrust at its neck. The monster howled with pain and rage, then turned at the end of its charge, and charged again. So the fight went on, until at length the Minotaur had received so many sword wounds that its strength began to fail. At last, with a blood-chilling groan it gave up the struggle and rolled on the ground, dead.

Hardly stopping to make sure that his victim breathed no more, Theseus searched for the end of the woollen thread, found it, and hurried back along the track by which he had come, twisting and turning until he found himself at the entrance of the labyrinth.

Great was the joy of his companions when they saw their leader return in triumph. They knew as soon as they saw the blood on his arms and tunic that he had been successful. While Theseus had been battling with the Minotaur,

Ariadne, having obtained the key by telling the guards a falsehood, had unlocked the door and greeted the young Athenians as they left the hated place. Then she hid them in a temple until the coming of dusk made it safe for them all to slip down to the harbour. Theseus thanked Ariadne for her help, and together they got aboard the ship in safety and hoisted sail.

The voyage began joyfully, for a favourable wind carried the ship swiftly over the blue waves away from the hated shores of Crete. The monster that had devoured so many of the youth of Athens was slain, and never again would the tribute have to be paid.

Then the wind changed, and the ship was carried towards the island of Naxos, where Theseus decided to put in for the night. The ship was made fast, and the Athenians, together with the Cretan princess, made their way ashore. Here

they feasted, and then lay down to rest. But during the night some god or goddess sent forgetfulness into the mind of Theseus, so that all thought of Ariadne was driven out of it. In his haste to return to Athens he forgot the princess who had helped him to save his companions, and whom he had promised to take home with him. Terrible was the grief of Ariadne when she rose soon after dawn and saw the ship far out to sea. She felt cruelly deserted, and for days went disconsolately up and down the shore weeping and calling upon the gods to save her from whatever destruction awaited her in that savage and inhospitable place.

Perhaps it was the god Dionysus who had made Theseus forgetful of his promise to Ariadne. For Dionysus had seen her from afar and fallen in love with her beauty. He determined to make her his bride. He was the god of feasting and merriment, of wine and laughter. In the depths of her

despair Ariadne was therefore amazed and delighted to hear the sounds of mirth and song as Dionysus and his companions came in a wild procession from the woods. The god was throned high in a chariot drawn by leopards, and behind him followed the goat-footed satyrs who were his train. Their brows were wreathed with vines and myrtle, the signs of merry-making, and over their shoulders hung great leathern bottles of wine. When the procession drew near to Ariadne, Dionysus leapt from his chariot and greeted her. They fell in love at first sight: the god lifted the princess into his chariot and carried her off to become his bride. So Ariadne soon forgot her grief at being deserted by Theseus.

Meanwhile in Athens Aegeus and all the people anxiously awaited the return of the ship. So eager was the old king to know the fate of his beloved son that he stood on the cliffs hour after hour, gazing towards the horizon. At last the ship came into view, but the triumph of Theseus's homecoming was dimmed by tragedy. For a second time the young hero forgot a promise. He had undertaken, if his mission were successful, to change the black sails for white, and this he had forgotten to do. On seeing the black sails looming nearer and nearer, Aegeus was overcome by unbearable grief. He knew – or thought he knew – that his son had been killed by the Cretan monster. With a great groan of anguish and despair, Aegeus rushed to the edge of the cliff and threw himself headlong into the waves. From that day to this the name of the sea in which the king drowned himself has been the Aegean.

Thus the end of Theseus's voyage was one of mingled sorrow and rejoicing – sorrow at his father's fate, and joy at the triumph of the hero who had saved the whole city from its terrible ordeal. After a due time of mourning, Theseus was crowned King of Athens, and so came into the birthright he had been promised in his earliest days in far Troizen.

Arion

Arion, a poet and musician, was the son of Oncaea and the sea-god Poseidon. His fame as a composer and performer on the lyre spread throughout Greece. He was celebrated as the inventor of a wild kind of song known as a dithyramb. People were drawn towards his music from far and near. Like Orpheus, he had the power to attract even animals with the strains of his music.

He became a favourite of King Periander of Corinth and spent much of his time at the court. Arrayed in his singing-robe of resplendent purple and gold, he would sweep the strings of his lyre and raise his voice in strange and tragic music which would silence even the most talkative of Periander's courtiers.

One day Arion said to his master:

'I hear there is to be a contest for musicians in the island of Sicily across the sea. I would dearly like to go and take part.'

'Stay here with me,' urged Periander. 'Sicily is a long way off. Those who strive for fame far from their native shores often come to disaster.'

'I am a poet,' said Arion, 'and the heart of a poet loves a wandering life. If I win the contest, I will come back covered with glory and will add new lustre to your court here in Corinth.'

'Besides,' Periander went on, 'I shall miss you. We shall all miss you and your music.'

'It will not be for long,' replied Arion. 'I will return as soon as the festival is over.'

So he went. It would take too long to say how he fared in Sicily. It is enough to know that he won the contest and received a handsome reward in gold and silver. So great was his prize that he was able to buy presents for Periander and all his friends in Corinth and have a great sum left for himself. With these he embarked on a ship bound for home. It was a ship belonging to Periander.

The sea was calm, the wind light, the sky a cloudless blue. Arion's heart rose high.

'Periander,' he cried, 'I shall soon be back home. You had no cause to fear. The voyage will have been a triumph, and my fortunes are made. What a splendid reunion we will have

as we sacrifice to the gods and especially to my father Poseidon and gather round the festive table to celebrate my triumph.'

But there was something he had forgotten – the treachery of greedy men. One day, while the ship still sailed smoothly on towards Greece, he chanced to overhear some of the sailors muttering among themselves. They knew of the great treasure he had aboard and were plotting to throw him into the sea and keep it for themselves. Before he had time to take in their words, they had gathered round him and were threatening his life.

'You must die, Arion,' said the leader of the sailors. 'If you wish to be buried on land, we will kill you here and take your body ashore with us. If you prefer a watery grave, throw yourself in the sea and swim for it.'

'Spare my life,' pleaded Arion, seeing that resistance was hopeless. 'Of what use is it to you? Take my treasure. I will give it to you freely in exchange for my life.'

They refused his request. They told him he must die. How could they live in safety to enjoy the treasure if Arion was alive to tell the tale?

In vain Arion pleaded with them, but they would not listen.

'Very well then,' he said gravely. 'Since I am to die, let me die as I have lived. Let me die the death of a poet and a singer. I will sing a last song to commend my soul to the gods. As soon as I have played and sung, I will yield myself up to you without complaint.'

They agreed, for a few of them indeed had sufficient curiosity to hear the voice of so famous a musician.

'Give me time to arrange my clothes,' said Arion, 'as befits this last act of mine, and tune the strings of my lyre in a manner suitable to one about to address the immortal gods.'

He put on his singing-robes of purple and gold and the

garlands of laurel he had won in Sicily. Then he took in his hands the lyre which he had played before kings and queens and tuned each of its strings for the performance of a death song. As he played his instrument and opened his lips in a great song of praise to the gods, gratitude for life and the desire of immortality, the sailors listened enchanted. All but the sternest nearly forgot their wicked purpose.

Then Arion strode to the edge of the deck and gazed down into the calm blue waters. Holding his lyre before him, he sang an address to it, unaccompanied by the sound of strings. 'O lyre,' he sang, 'come with me on my last journey. You who have been the companion of my life shall not be parted from me in death. Together we will make the journey to the dread shores, where the happy souls rest in peace after the turmoil of life. Together we shall charm the dreaded Cerberus who guards the doors of Hades, and we shall not fear to cross the dark river of death. There we shall see Orpheus himself, whose lyre calmed even the terrible Furies. There we shall meet all the great and famous poets whose music has been silenced on earth. As for those who are sending us on this last solemn journey, the time of their destruction shall surely come!'

So saying, he turned on the sailors with a look of triumph, raised his lyre in the air and sprang overboard into the deep sea. When Arion had sunk beneath the waves, the men tightened sail and made haste to continue on their way. Now, they imagined, they were safe. Their victim was drowned, and none should know of their wickedness, supposing the disappearance of Arion to have been an accident. They could enjoy the fruits of their crime in peace.

But Arion was not drowned. While he had been singing on the deck, the inhabitants of the deep had gathered around to listen – water-nymphs, dolphins, and all the fish of the

sea. So when Arion was struggling to keep his head above water, he found himself surrounded by dolphins. He grasped at one of them and pulled himself up on its back. Here he rode safely on the surface of the ocean and was soon brought to the shore. At the place where he landed, a monument was afterwards put up, on which was carved the figure of the poet, lyre in hand, riding upon the dolphin's back. In this way future travellers would remember the famous poet whose life had been marvellously preserved.

Arion gazed out to sea after the retreating dolphin, giving thanks to the gods for his deliverance. Then he left the seashore behind him and returned to Corinth. As he journeyed towards the city as swiftly as his legs would take him, he struck the chords of his lyre and raised his voice in a song of happiness and thanksgiving.

Soon he entered the royal palace and was greeted enthusiastically by King Periander.

'My friend and master,' Arion said, 'I have come back to you laden with honour, but not, alas, with treasure. I was victorious in the contest, but evil men have stolen the gifts I had brought for you. I have been stripped of all I own. I have nothing but my lyre, my singing-robes and my fame.'

Periander listened with astonishment and anger while Arion recounted all that had happened to him.

'We must catch these knaves,' he said, 'and punish them as they deserve. Your dolphin must have travelled fast, for no ship has come into harbour from Sicily since you left.'

It was agreed that Arion should remain privately at the palace and that nothing should be said about his return. As soon as the ship came into harbour, Periander had the sailors brought before him. Silently they stood facing the well-guarded figure of the King as he sat on his throne before great embroidered curtains of purple wool.

'I have sent for you,' said the King pleasantly, 'to ask if you saw or heard anything of Arion the musician when you were in Sicily. We await his return.'

The men looked crafty, as their leader stepped forward and said:

'Yes, your Majesty, we heard much of his fame in Sicily, and when we set sail for home he was being praised and feasted by all the great ones of the land. He was in the best of health and spirits.'

Then from between the curtains behind the throne stepped Arion, staring in triumph upon the sailors. He appeared exactly as they had last seen him, arrayed in his singing-robes, his wreath of woven laurel, his lyre in his hand. Instantly the sailors fell at the feet of Periander and Arion, groaning and begging for mercy.

'We meant to murder him,' said one. 'But he has become a god and has been saved from drowning. Otherwise he could not appear in living form. May the earth open and take our worthless bodies.'

'Arion is no god,' said Periander, eyeing the wretched men sternly, 'but he has been saved by the help of the gods. My poet has been restored to me. He does not seek your lives, for he is without the spirit of revenge. Better men than you have been tempted to murder by the greed for gold. You shall not be put to death, as you deserve. Instead, when you have restored what you took from your helpless passenger, leave my country, never to return. Find some barbarous land, fitted for thieves and murderers and pass the rest of your days in honest work and true repentance.'

When the sailors had been led away by the guards, Periander turned to Arion and said:

'Fame is good, but the pursuit of it may bring disaster. How fortunate it was that the dolphins have an ear for music. Now let us prepare for the banquet, and after it you shall tune your lyre and sing as you never sang before – not even at the festival in Sicily.'

The Fall of Troy

For ten years the Greeks had been trying in vain to capture the city of Troy, which lay across the sea. Paris, the son of Priam, King of Troy, had carried off a Greek queen, the beautiful Helen. Her husband, Menelaus, had roused many of the Greek kings and chieftains to gather an army together. They collected many ships and sailed to the coast near Troy. Then they besieged the city and tried to force their way in. For ten long years the war went on. Many brave men were killed on both sides. The Greek warriors began to fear they could never win. But the war came to an end at last, and this is the story of how it happened.

The guardian goddess of Troy was Pallas Athene. There were many statues to her set up in temples in the city, and of these the most famous and the most precious was known as the Palladium. It was thought to have fallen from heaven and so to be a gift from the gods themselves. The Trojans believed that the city could never be taken so long as the Palladium was safe inside its walls.

Then one dark night when all Troy was asleep, and the towers and palaces were lit only by starlight, two bold Greeks, Odysseus and Diomedes, stole silently into Troy, carried off the precious statue and took it back to their camp. The Greeks well knew how greatly their enemies prized the Palladium.

But in spite of the loss of the statue Troy still held out. The Greeks called a council of war and decided that, since they could not take the city by force, they must do it by trickery. This was the advice of the cunning leader Odysseus. They pretended that they were giving up the fight and sailing home. Some of the ships set sail and left the coast, only to anchor a short distance away behind a near-by island called Tenedos. Some of the Greeks remained behind in their camp on the plains between the sea and the city. Then they built from fir wood a gigantic horse, which they left well within sight of the Trojans. This done, they carried away their tents and equipment and sailed away to join the rest of the fleet moored behind Tenedos. Next morning the Trojan guards reported with amazement that the Greeks were nowhere to be seen. Their camp was broken up, the ships vanished. Great was the rejoicing as the gates of the city were opened and the citizens poured out. They wandered freely over the deserted battlefields of the past ten years, gazing with wonder at their enemy's old encampment. It all seemed too marvellous to be true.

What excited their liveliest curiosity was the wooden horse. Everyone tried to guess what it was for. Most thought it was a sign of surrender, or a peace offering, or else perhaps an image for the gods to ensure a safe return for the Greek ships.

'Let us take it into the city!' cried some. 'Let us set it up in our market-place as a memorial to our dead and a sign of victory to be shown to our children and grandchildren.'

'Yes,' echoed others. 'Into the city with the horse!'

'Fetch wheels and ropes and drag it in triumph through our gates!'

Then Laocoön, the priest of the sea-god Poseidon, who was on his way to make a morning sacrifice to the god, raised his hand for silence and called out sternly:

'Are you mad, fellow-Trojans? Never trust the Greeks. This is some trick. Have you fought them for ten years only to be beaten by cunning? I am no coward, but I am afraid of all Greeks, especially when they bring gifts.'

With these words he aimed his spear at the horse's side. The point pierced it, and a hollow sound came from within. It seemed as if Laocoön had persuaded the Trojans to his way of thinking, for some prepared to destroy the Greek offering there and then,

'He is right,' said someone. 'Let us burn the thing!'

But at that moment a group of Trojans appeared, dragging with them a terrified Greek who had been left behind and had been found hiding among the bushes near the seashore. The man, whose hands had been tied behind his back, was brought before King Priam and the other Trojan leaders.

'Spare my life, I beg,' pleaded the prisoner. 'Or if you will not, then give me a quick and merciful death.'

'We will spare your life,' said the King, 'on condition that you answer our questions truthfully.'

The man promised to tell them all they wanted to know, and his hands were untied.

'I am a Greek,' he said in answer to their questions, 'by name Sinon. The Greeks have sailed for home. The decision to give up the war was taken after long and bitter discussion. It was agreed to make a human sacrifice to the gods on their departure to make sure of a fortunate voyage. Because Odysseus hated me, he persuaded the leaders that I, Sinon, was to be the victim. However, last night I managed to escape and hide near the shore. My countrymen are now my enemies, as they have been yours. All I ask is to be allowed to live among you and become a citizen of Troy – or only a slave, if you so decide.'

Sinon looked so humble and so piteous that no one doubted his words.

'And what,' asked Priam, 'is the purpose of this monstrous image?'

Sinon told the Trojans that the Greeks had left the horse as an offering to the goddess Athena.

'But why did it have to be of this enormous size?'

'Ah,' replied the crafty Sinon, 'it was made huge so that you would not be able to bring it inside your gates. One of our prophets said that if you managed to get the horse inside the city, no one would ever be able to conquer Troy. You would be safe so long as the wooden horse was within your walls.'

All who heard the Greek were deeply impressed. Surely this unfortunate man was speaking the truth. They were beginning to think of ways by which they might drag the monster through the gates of the city when a terrible event

occurred – an event which made them hesitate no longer.

Their priest Laocoön, with his two little sons, was on his way to the shore to make his offering to Poseidon when two huge serpents appeared from the sea and advanced directly towards him. All gasped with horror as the scaly creatures wound themselves round the bodies of the boys and crushed them to death. Their father, struggling hopelessly to free the boys, was himself wrapped round by the serpents' coils, so that he could no longer breathe and fell lifeless to the ground beside the bodies of the children. A cry of horror went up from the people.

'He has angered the gods,' they said, 'and this is their revenge. He struck the horse with his spear, and they sent the sea-serpents to kill him. Now we know that the image is sacred, and the Greek is speaking the truth.'

Some of the Trojans fetched wheels and ropes and hauled the wooden horse to the gates of the city. Others, meanwhile, took down one of the gateposts and part of the wall which supported it, so as to make room for its passage. Then, with songs of triumph, they pulled it right to the very heart of Troy, where it stood in the market-place towering over the people. They danced about it, strewing flowers before it and throwing garlands about its neck. Then, as evening fell, the people prepared to feast and make merry. Drinking and singing, they roamed about the streets until, worn out with the day's excitements, they went home and slept a sounder sleep than they had enjoyed for ten years. Their enemies had gone, and the wooden horse would keep their city safe.

But Laocoön had been right to mistrust the Greeks, for the

horse was no offering to the gods but a means of destruction. Inside its hollow sides were a score or more of the bravest of the Greek warriors. They had been waiting there, fully armed, all that day and the whole of the night before. Sinon, who had taken care to hide near the horse, now crept out of the shadows, gave his friends the signal and let them out of their hiding-place. Swiftly they climbed down the rope ladder they had taken inside the horse and made their way to the city gates.

The breach in the wall had been repaired by the Trojans as soon as the horse was inside, and the gates had been closed and barred. But the sentries, fearing no ill, had fallen asleep after their merrymaking, and the Greek warriors had no difficulty in overpowering them. Meanwhile, under cover of night the main body of the Greeks had returned from their shelter behind the island of Tenedos, and were now gathered outside the gates, waiting for their friends to let them in.

Then began the utter destruction of Priam's beautiful city. As the terrified Trojans awoke from sleep, they heard the crackling of flames, the clash of arms and the shouting of the exultant Greeks. Their enemies rushed from street to street, burning, looting and pulling down. The men of Troy hastily buckled on their armour, helped by their panic-stricken women; they went out, sword in hand, to battle with the Greeks. Spears and lances flew through the air. Even the boys fought. As the flames took hold of the lofty buildings, roofs and gables caught fire, and stone towers toppled upon the heads of attackers and defenders alike. Dogs rushed shrieking through the streets, driven mad by the flames. Girls cowered inside the houses, trying to quieten their baby brothers and sisters, until driven out by fire or the enemy.

The Trojans, taken by surprise, were no match for the

Greeks. They were put to the sword, while the women were carried off to be slaves. Yet many of the Greeks were slain too. Many of the sons of King Priam were killed or taken prisoner; Priam himself was slain as he took refuge in the temple of Athene.

So ended the great and proud kingdom of Troy, and the city became a smoking ruin, a scene of death and desolation. The Greeks withdrew to their ships and set sail for home, carrying away their slaves and their booty, the treasures of Troy's temples and palaces. Thus ended the ten years' war in a single night.

Odysseus and Polyphemus

After the Trojan war the Greek warriors who had taken part in it returned home. Odysseus and his companions set sail in a number of ships and made towards the island of Ithaca, of which he was the ruler. But storms arose and drove the ships off their course. On they went, day after day, getting no nearer home. Before their voyage was done, they had weathered many gales and experienced many adventures. One of the first of these was their visit to the island of the Cyclopes.

These were a tribe of giants, and they were now the sole inhabitants of their island. The word Cyclops means 'the Round-Eyed One'. Each of the giants had only one eye, placed in the middle of his forehead. Not only were the Cyclopes of enormous size, they were rough and shaggy. They were shepherds, living on mutton and on other foods they found on their island. They dwelt in caves.

When Odysseus approached the island, he was in need of rest and refreshment. So he left most of his ships at anchor near by and sailed his own close in. He and his crew went ashore to spy out the land, taking a large earthenware jar of wine as a present to the natives.

Not far inland they found a deep cave. It belonged to Polyphemus, one of the strongest and biggest of the Cyclopes. It was this Polyphemus who, when young, had fallen in love with the beautiful sea-nymph Galatea. He had pursued her, singing rough songs in his huge rumbling voice. But this only frightened her. Then he would sit for hours among his enormous rams, playing on a pipe he had made of a hundred reeds. This too had displeased the nymph.

She was, indeed, in love with a handsome young shepherd called Acis. One day Acis was lying in the mouth of a cave under the cliffs wooing Galatea with soft words when they heard the raucous tones of the Cyclops bawling songs of lamentation as he sat on a promontory near the sea. He was far enough away, but his voice carried like the noise of thunder among the mountains.

Then Polyphemus, restless and unhappy, strode to the top of a rock, where his sheep, to which he paid small attention, followed him. Then he threw down his staff, the trunk of a young pine-tree, took out his reed-pipe and began to play.

Suddenly, casting his eye about him, he caught sight of Galatea in the arms of Acis. This was too much for the lovesick giant. He jumped to his feet and roared out:

'Aha! I see you, cruel maiden! You are happy with your shepherd, but I will make sure this is the last time you and he make love together!'

The sound of the Cyclops's voice so terrified Galatea that she jumped up in alarm and sprang into the sea. Only a ripple was left to show where she had dived in.

Acis, too, rose up in alarm and tried to run away. But Polyphemus, with huge strides, followed him, tearing off a boulder from the mountainside as he did so. This he threw with all his force at the retreating shepherd. The

giant's aim was good, and Acis was buried beneath the rock.

But the gods took pity on him. From the earth there gushed first red blood, then muddy water. Then the rock split open, and a tall green reed rose up. Next a clear, sparkling spring appeared, the river god standing in its cool waters. So was born a new river, and to this day it is called the Acis. As for Polyphemus, he left that country and went back to his own people. He never took a wife, nor did he ever again play on his pipes or sing love-songs. Silent and disconsolate, he brooded alone in his cave or among his flocks in the hills.

When Odysseus and his companions came to the cave, the owner was away, tending his sheep. They entered it and found it stocked with fine, fat sheep, lambs and kids, cheeses and bowls of milk. Presently the master of the cave returned. Odysseus and his men were well hidden inside the cave. From their hiding-place they saw Polyphemus drive his flocks in, throw down a pile of firewood and then close the mouth of the cave by rolling into it a huge boulder. This he did with scarcely an effort, but it would have taken twenty oxen to move it. Next Polyphemus sat down upon a stout wooden stool and milked the sheep. He set aside part of the milk to make cheese, and the rest he kept in a bowl for his supper.

At last he turned round. With his glaring eye he saw the strangers – Odysseus and his sailors hiding in the rear of the cave.

'Who are you?' he roared in a monstrous voice. 'And what are you doing here?'

'We are Greeks, sir,' answered Odysseus respectfully. 'We have taken part in the long war against Troy. Now we are returning home, and our ship has been driven on to this island. We seek rest, food and shelter. In the name of the gods who are above us all, we beg the favour of your hospitality.'

The giant made no reply but slowly rose from his stool and approached the men. Then with his huge brawny arms and enormous hands he seized two of them and flung them crashing against the wall of the cave. The others were horrified to see their luckless companions murdered in cold blood. They were still more horrified to see the giant devour them, tearing them apart with his bare hands. Then Polyphemus washed down his meal with a bowl of milk, stretched himself out and lay on the floor of the cave to sleep.

'Kill him, master,' said one of the sailors in a hoarse whisper. 'He's asleep. Stick your sword into his heart before he can wake.'

'I am sorely tempted to do it,' answered Odysseus. 'But if

we kill him now, we shall never escape. We shall die here miserably once we have eaten all the cheese and drunk all the milk. How can we ever hope to shift that enormous rock and get out of the cave alive? We are imprisoned unless the giant himself moves the rock.'

Sadly the sailors agreed that Odysseus was right. They made a meal of cheese and milk and lay down to sleep.

Next morning Polyphemus stretched his great hairy body, yawned and rose to his feet. Then he seized two more of Odysseus's shrinking companions and served them as he had served the others, devouring their lifeless bodies with relish. When he had finished his grisly breakfast, he rolled back the rock and drove his sheep and goats out to pasture. Before he left, he was careful to push the rock back into position, so as to keep his visitors imprisoned until his return.

While he was away, Odysseus sat down to work out a plan for getting the better of their enemy and escaping from their dreadful prison. He made his men sharpen the end of a huge wooden pole which the giant had brought into the cave as a staff and hardened the point in the fire. Then they hid it under the straw at the back of the cave.

Towards nightfall the giant returned as before with his flock, milked them and prepared for supper. Once more he seized two of Odysseus's companions and made his supper of them. Then Odysseus came forward and offered him a bowl of wine.

'Drink it, Cyclops,' he said. 'It will taste good and refresh you after your meal of human flesh.'

Polyphemus grabbed the bowl of wine and greedily drank it down at a single gulp.

Odysseus gave him more. The giant grinned to show his pleasure.

'That is good,' he said. 'Thank you for this. I will keep you

till the end and not eat you until I have eaten all the others. What is your name?'

'My name,' answered the cunning Odysseus, 'is Noman.'

Drowsy with the strong wine, Polyphemus was soon fast asleep, snoring like distant thunder. At once Odysseus and four chosen companions fetched out the sharpened pole from under the straw and made it red-hot in the embers of the fire. It burned and glowed and crackled. Then the five of them stood above the sleeping giant, raised the pole high in the air and, at a signal from Odysseus, drove it deep into the giant's only eye. They twirled it in the socket as a carpenter twirls his gimlet. As the monster, howling with pain, woke and jumped to his feet, they sprang out of reach, joining their companions at the farther end of the cave. Polyphemus groaning and bellowing, lunged blindly here and there, knocking himself against the walls and stumbling over boulders, arousing the frightened animals with his cries and making them bleat piteously. Never had such a din been heard in the island of the Cyclopes. The other giants from neighbouring caves came running towards the dwelling of Polyphemus, shouting:

'What is the matter, Polyphemus, that you bawl out in this way and wake us from our slumbers?'

'I am hurt,' he called. 'I have been blinded and I shall die of the pain.'

'Who has hurt you?' they called.

'Noman,' replied Polyphemus. 'Noman has hurt me.'

'Then if no man has hurt you,' they answered, 'it must be the will of the gods, and we can do nothing for you. We cannot alter the will of Zeus.'

Then the other giants departed and left Polyphemus to his groaning.

Next morning the Cyclops rolled away the stone from the mouth of the cave to let out his flocks. He could not see, so, to be sure that Odysseus and his men did not escape, he stood by the wall of the entrance to make sure they did not pass him. But cunning Odysseus had made his men yoke the sheep together, three by three, using strands of willow that had been brought into the cave to make baskets for the giant's cheeses. Under the belly of the middle sheep hung a Greek, clinging to the animal's fleece. Polyphemus felt the backs and sides of the outermost sheep, in case the Greeks should be riding on their backs, but he did not think of feeling their bellies. So all the Greeks passed out of the giant's cave. Odysseus himself came out last.

As soon as the men were clear of the cave, they jumped down from under the sheep and made for the boat, driving as many of the sheep as possible before them. They intended to keep them on board for food during the voyage. As soon as they were safely in the boat, they pushed out to sea.

When they were a safe distance from the shore, Odysseus, standing on the deck, looked towards the sightless giant near the water's edge and called out:

'Cyclops, the gods have punished you for your vile cruelty towards a helpless band of Greeks. Know you, Cyclops, that it was I, Odysseus of Ithaca, who planned and carried out the act which blinded you and gave us our freedom.'

For answer the enraged Polyphemus wrenched a mighty rock from the ground, raised it on high with his two mighty arms and hurled it with all his strength towards the voice he had heard. The rock rose high in the air, narrowly missed the ship's mainmast and crashed into the water just beyond the vessel. So huge was the wave thus caused that the ship was driven back towards the island and beached itself once more in the sand. The men were hard put to it to drive the ship once more out to sea. Once more Odysseus was about to address the monster, but his friends persuaded him to wait till they were farther from the land. As soon as they were at a safe distance, the Greeks raised their voices in a great shout, to let Polyphemus know that they had escaped his vengeance.

Then they hoisted sail, bent their backs to the oars and made off as fast as they could to rejoin the other ships.

Odysseus and Circe

Odysseus and his men sailed on, caring only to reach their homes on the isle of Ithaca. When there was a good breeze, they hoisted the sails and sped over the blue waves. When there was no wind, they bent their backs to the oars and pulled sturdily. The voyage was long and weary. They had many times been driven off their course, and Odysseus decided to ask for the help of the god Aeolus, in whose keeping were all the winds that blow. So he steered his ship towards the island where Aeolus lived, and the other ships followed. Next day they put in at the harbour, and Odysseus went up to the palace of King Aeolus. The King and his family were feasting. The traveller was hospitably entertained, and next morning Aeolus gave him a leather bag whose mouth was tied with a thong. It bulged with all the winds. Odysseus was told to release only the west wind, and this would drive his ship home. He thanked the King, rejoined his men, weighed anchor and set off. He kept the bag beside him, and himself managed the helm. Then he carefully opened the bulging bag and let out only the west wind. Gradually the sails filled, and the ship bounded over the waves.

For several days the ship rode on. Odysseus alone managed the helm, so fearful was he that they might go off course. At length he became weary and, almost within sight of his

native land, he lay down on the deck and fell fast asleep. The moon came out and shone on the sleeping form of the leader and on the bulging leather bag he kept beside him.

The sailors gathered round and began talking in undertones.

'I'd like to know what the old man has in that bag,' said one of them.

'Mark my words,' said another, 'that King – Aeolus, wasn't it? – gave him some treasure to take home, and that's what's in the bag.'

'Yes, shouldn't wonder. He's going to keep it all to himself. We'll ask him for a share of it.'

'First, let's look inside and make sure what it is. Gold and silver and precious stones, I shouldn't wonder.'

'Come on then. Undo the bag. Do it quietly or you'll wake him.'

Then the sailor nearest to Odysseus drew out a sharp knife and cut the cord that bound the neck of the bag. Instantly all the other winds rushed out with a mighty roar, and Odysseus awoke to find the ship tossing madly in all directions.

'Fools!' he cried. 'What have you done? You have ruined everything, and we shall be destroyed by storms. Quick, lower the sails. Get to your stations and man the oars.'

But it was too late. Already the sails were filled with a great wind from the north-east. The ship rocked and pitched. The men had strength only to lower the smaller of the sails. They were driven violently back towards the island of Aeolus, which they had left only a few days earlier.

Odysseus made the men take the ship into harbour, and once more he sought the help of Aeolus. But the King spoke to him sternly.

'No,' he said. 'I dare not help you further. The gods are against you. This is proved by your falling asleep when at the helm and allowing your men to act recklessly. You must continue your journey without my help.'

Once more they set out, but now the winds failed and the sails hung idly, flapping against the masts. The men were obliged to use the oars. At length, weary and discouraged, they put in at the island of the Laestrygonians in search of food and water. These were a race of cannibal giants, as savage and barbarous as the Cyclopes. Some of the ships went right into the harbour, but Odysseus wisely remained in open water outside. As soon as the giants saw the ships, they seized great rocks and hurled them over the cliffs, smashing two or three of the ships to fragments. As rock after rock crashed down on the decks, the sailors could do nothing except scramble into the water and make for the shore as best they could. Here the cruel Laestrygonians speared them from above, so that none was left alive. Seeing that he could do nothing to help them, Odysseus gave orders to his crew to row for their lives and get as far away as possible from the accursed island.

In course of time the ship reached the island of Aeaea, where lived the enchantress Circe, bright-haired daughter of the sun. Here on the shore Odysseus and his men rested for two days. There was no sign of life on the island, so Odysseus climbed a high hill not far inland to spy out the country. He saw no human habitations except one. This was a fair palace standing in a glade among trees in the centre of the island. He returned to the shore and told his men what he had discovered. Then he divided the party into two – one under his own command, the other under the command of Eurylochus. The two leaders drew lots as to which should go first and make himself known at the palace. The lot fell

to Eurylochus, who with his men set off towards the centre of the island. Odysseus and his party awaited their return.

When Eurylochus and his men reached the grove where stood the palace, they were surrounded by lions and wolves. In terror some of them turned to run. Others drew their spears and prepared to fight. But to their amazement the beasts were all tame, fawning upon them and licking their hands and faces, as a dog greets his master after a long absence.

The reason was this. The beasts had all been men, but they had been changed by the magic power of the enchantress Circe. They had the forms of lions and wolves, but their hearts and minds were still those of men.

Encouraged by this, the party approached the gates of the palace. Within they heard the sound of sweet music and of women's voices. Then the bright-haired queen herself came out and beckoned them inside. All went in except Eurylochus. He was afraid and waited outside the gate.

Circe bade the men be seated at a long table in her hall. Then she had servants place before them delicate food and strong wine. The men feasted and drank as they had never done before. As they did so, Circe walked back and forth before her great loom, weaving a cloth of rich dyes and mysterious design, singing to herself in her high, unearthly voice.

Then, when she saw that her guests were half asleep with eating and drinking, she took up a golden wand of delicate workmanship and touched each of them lightly on the shoulder, muttering an incantation in some strange tongue. Instantly each of the sailors was turned into a pig. Grunting and jostling each other, they ran about the hall. Their flapping ears, bristly skins and curved tusks were those of pigs, but their hearts and minds remained their own. Circe summoned her swineherds who, with sharp sticks drove the

squealing beasts into sties at the rear of the palace. Here they were penned in and fed on beechnuts and acorns and the swill from the kitchens.

Seeing all this, Eurylochus, in fear and sorrow, sped back to the shore to tell their leader what had happened.

'Where are your companions?' asked Odysseus as soon as he saw Eurylochus. 'What has become of my men?'

'Oh master,' cried Eurylochus with tears in his eyes, 'a terrible thing has befallen them!' Then with horror and despair making his tale more piteous, he described all he had seen.

At once Odysseus set off alone to see what he could do to deliver his men from their terrible captivity. In vain Eurylochus pleaded with him not to go, or at least to take some trusted companion. But Odysseus, as brave as he was cunning, set off alone.

Halfway to the palace he met a young man of pleasing appearance who greeted him and begged speech with him.

'You are the famous Odysseus, I know,' said the youth, 'and you are on your way home after serving the Greeks at Troy.'

Then the young man said he was Hermes, messenger of the gods, who had bidden him find out Odysseus and be of service to him in his journey.

'Circe,' he told Odysseus, 'is an enchantress of great power and she has changed your men into beasts, just as you have been told. She will do the same to you, and I advise you to get as far from her as you can and put as many sea miles as possible between you and her island.'

'No,' said Odysseus firmly. 'I brought the men here, and it is for me to do what I can to rescue them.'

'Very well,' said Hermes. 'Since you are determined to face the enchantress, listen to me carefully. Gather some of this herb you see growing about you – the one with the black root and the white flower, called moly. Keep it with you when you encounter the witch, and it will protect you against her enchantments. When she attempts to bewitch you, you must rush at her with your sword drawn and make as if to cut her throat. When she is at your mercy, she will agree to do all you ask. Now do as I say, and may the gods protect you.'

Odysseus thanked the young man and went on his way. He boldly entered the courtyard of the palace and stood before the entrance. Circe, the bright-haired daughter of the sun god, her heart dark with mischief, welcomed him in and treated him courteously, bidding him be seated at her table. Servants brought him food and wine, and she entertained him by singing before her loom. Then, when he had feasted and drunk, she stepped swiftly towards him, touched him on the shoulder with her golden wand and said in a shrill, inhuman voice:

'There, stranger! Now go to the sty and eat with your fellow-swine!'

But Odysseus grew no long bristles, nor did he grunt and squeal. Instead, he drew his sharp sword, brandished it over the enchantress and stared into her face with a look of fury. The sorceress was beaten. She went down on her knees, raised her hands towards him and begged to be allowed to live.

'Very well,' said Odysseus. 'On one condition. Repeat after me this oath.'

Then she swore to restore Odysseus's companions to their former manly shape, entertain them hospitably and without doing them further harm, and finally let them go in peace and security.

'You are Odysseus,' she said when she had sworn the oath. 'Hermes came and told me to expect you. I will release your sailors and you shall all be entertained at my palace for as long as you wish to stay.'

At once the men who had been turned into pigs were changed back into men. They looked even younger and more handsome than before. Odysseus went back to the shore to summon the others to the palace. Eurylochus was still afraid and wished to remain behind. but Odysseus would not let him.

'Come,' he said. 'All is now safe. Let us eat and drink at the queen's expense and pass our days in ease and pleasure.'

Circe did all that she had promised. Odysseus and his men were royally entertained, and for many days they stayed with her. They roamed the island, playing games amongst themselves or swimming in the blue sea as if they had no cares in the world. They feasted and drank to their hearts' content, and Circe practised no further enchantments upon them. It seemed as if Odysseus had forgotten his home and the purpose of his voyage.

At last Eurylochus and some of the others reminded him that they had wives and children who had been waiting for their return for many long years. Odysseus agreed to bid farewell to the enchantress. She parted from him with tears of farewell in her eyes, giving him instructions for the next stage of his journey. In particular she warned him of the

dangers that awaited him when he should pass the island of the Sirens. Then one bright morning when the wind was favourable, Odysseus made sacrifice to the gods and boarded his ship. The men hoisted sail, weighed anchor and watched the island of Aeaea grow smaller in the distance.

Not long afterwards Odysseus knew that the ship was approaching the Sirens, so he ordered everything to be done as Circe had advised. The island, he was told, was surrounded by treacherous and jagged rocks, on which a ship might be wrecked and a swimmer torn to pieces. On the shores of this island lay the Sirens, maidens of great beauty not unlike the mermaids of later legends. As they combed their long flowing hair, they sang songs of such unearthly sweetness that no man who heard them could resist their magic. Some played on stringed instruments made from great sea-shells. All raised their voices in strains of unrivalled harmony, not heard elsewhere by human ears. Many was the good ship which had been steered on to the rocks by men unable to sail past the Sirens' island; many were the young sailors who had leaped into the sea and been torn to pieces on the hidden rocks, so that whitening bones and fragments of wreckage were to be seen all along the shore as a warning to desperate and foolish mariners. Those relics should have spoken plainly to all, but Circe had urged Odysseus to take no risks.

He told the men to fill their ears with wax, so that they should not hear the song of the Sirens. As for him, he stood with his back to the mainmast and his eyes towards the shore, while his men bound him to the mast with ropes. On no account were they to obey him if he should tell them to release him. He was to remain bound to the mast so long as the island was within sight and sound.

No sooner were these preparations complete than they came in sight of the shore, edged with the bones of sailors and tall ships. On the beaches lay the Sirens, some combing their hair, others plucking the strings of their lyres. All sang. The mariners saw everything but heard nothing. Their leader alone was allowed to listen to the ravishing strains of their music, as they beckoned to him with song and gesture to come and taste the joys of their island. He was seized with an overwhelming desire to sail nearer. Sweating and straining, he heaved at the ropes till they cut into his flesh and he cried out in pain. Then he signalled to the men to come and cut the cords. But they obeyed his earlier command and brought more ropes to lash him still faster to the mast. It seemed as if the mast would crack with the strain. Then at last, out of breath from his exertions, he relaxed and leaned back, his ears filled with the Sirens' music, till it grew fainter and fainter as the ship swung past the fatal shore and the gleaming beaches, and the maidens and their songs were lost in the distance.

When the place was no more than a speck on the horizon, Odysseus ordered the crew to release him and take the wax from their ears. Thus one more danger was passed on the long voyage back to Ithaca from the ruined city of Troy.

Scylla and Charybdis

Before Odysseus left the island of the enchantress Circe, she warned him of a further danger they would encounter. Soon they would have to pass through a narrow strait between high cliffs. On one side was a whirlpool named Charybdis. It boiled and hissed and threw up great spouts of foam. As the angry water swirled over the bottomless chasm, it sought, like some devouring monster, to suck into its gulf any boat or ship that passed too close. Many poor sailors and fine vessels, passing too near the dreadful whirlpool, had been dragged into its depths and lost for ever. But if a ship sailed too close to the opposite shore of the strait, it ran into an equally terrible danger. This was the monster Scylla, who lived in a cave high up in the cliffs opposite the whirlpool. Scylla had been a beautiful maiden, but Circe had changed her into a snaky creature with six heads. In each of her mouths stood two rows of sharp teeth, and it was her habit to reach down her serpent necks whenever a ship passed within reach and seize as many of the crew as she could. She carried them into her cave and devoured them with hideous delight. Many brave men had met their end in this manner.

Odysseus's ship had not long been sailing from Circe's island when there rose into view the spray and steam from the whirlpool Charybdis. Odysseus had warned them of this danger, and they now became panic-stricken, so that the blades of their oars fell upon the water, and they could no longer row.

'Take heart, men!' cried Odysseus. 'This danger is no worse than what we faced in the cave of Polyphemus. I brought you safely out of that, and we shall live to tell our children of how we escaped from the whirlpool. Keep close into the farther shore and row your hardest.'

So the sailors took heart, gripped their oars and pulled hard for the entrance to the strait, steering close in to the shore farthest from the whirlpool. But Odysseus had not dared to tell them of the peril that lay in wait on this side. If he had told them of Scylla, he was afraid they would lose heart altogether, drop their oars and hide themselves below deck. They must be made to row hard through the narrow passage, come what might.

Circe had forbidden Odysseus to arm himself, for, she said, the monster was irresistible. With her six heads and writhing, snaky necks she could never be destroyed. But this command was too much for a fighter, so Odysseus buckled on his armour, took up two spears and stood on the prow of the ship to get a sight of the monster. In vain he strained his eyes, trying to discover her cave high in the cliff.

Nearer and nearer sailed the ship towards the narrowest part of the passage. As it reached the whirlpool, the men did not flinch, but rowed hard, as Odysseus had told them. They felt the pull of the water, and as they neared the deadly gulf, they could see right down its spinning sides to the sand and rocks beneath. They shuddered, and the steersman held his course near the farther cliffs. It was then that Scylla thrust her six heads out of the cave and seized six of the sailors with her horrible fangs. Their companions were terrified to see them raised screaming into the air,

struggling hopelessly to free themselves from Scylla's grip. Their efforts were in vain. Writhing and screaming and calling upon their leader and the gods to help them for the last time, they vanished into the cave, where the ravening beast devoured them. This was the most horrible event which took place during the whole of Odysseus's journey.

Sad at heart, but thankful to be out of reach of Scylla and Charybdis, Odysseus and his men sailed out of the narrow waters into the open sea. Soon they could make out on the horizon the island of the sun god, of which Circe had told Odysseus. She had warned him on no account to land there, however tempted he might be, for the island was sacred to the golden cattle of the sun. It was death to any man who should injure these cattle. Nearer and nearer they came to the lovely island. Soon they could see its golden sands and hospitable coves with vines and olives coming

almost down to the water's edge. Further inland were rich
meadows where the golden cattle browsed peacefully, now
and again raising their heads to low contentedly.

The tired eyes of the sailors rested hungrily on these sights.
Sternly Odysseus told them they might not land but must
sail on.

Then the men began to grumble and protest. Angrily
Eurylochus spoke out:

'Odysseus, are you a man of flesh and blood or a stone
statue? After our terrible journey between the whirlpool and
the six-headed monster are we to have no rest?'

'It is the command of the gods,' said Odysseus sternly.

'Night is coming on,' Eurylochus replied. 'Let us anchor
here at least till morning. We cannot struggle on through
the darkness. How if a storm should arise and smash us to
pieces or drive us back into the cruel straits?'

All the crew loudly supported Eurylochus, and with a heart full of foreboding Odysseus was forced to consent. But he made them swear an oath to the immortal gods that they would on no account touch the golden cattle, the sacred cattle of the sun. So they beached the ship, drew water from a clear spring and sat down on the shore to eat the food they had brought. Then at last, overcome by weariness and by grief at the loss of their six friends, they fell asleep.

A little after midnight the sky suddenly became covered with a thick cloud, so that the stars were blotted out and a fierce storm arose. It was just as Eurylochus had feared. Odysseus roused his men, and together they dragged the ship high on shore to be out of reach of the rising storm, for he feared it might be dashed to pieces. The wind had changed and for a whole month it blew hard from the wrong quarter. They dared not put to sea.

Before long they had eaten all the provisions in the ship and began to snare birds and catch fish to keep themselves alive. It was a sparse diet, for the weather made it hard to get enough of either birds or fish. Some of the men began to think of the fat beasts that would be theirs to roast if only they dare break their oath not to harm the golden cattle.

Odysseus, perplexed and anxious, went to a quiet place away from the others in order to pray to the gods for help. Sleep fell upon him, and before he awoke, Eurylochus had given his companions bad counsel.

'Friends,' he said, 'we have sworn not to touch the cattle. But if we do not, we shall starve. No man could live on what we are able to catch. We are all ill with hunger. Before we have not strength enough left, let us kill the fattest of the cows and make a sacrifice to the gods. Then, if we reach home, we can build a temple to the sun god as an offering for our safe return and to calm his anger at our disobedience.

But even if he wrecks our ship in revenge, it would be better to die a quick death by drowning than slowly starve within sight and sound of food.'

All agreed, and without further argument they killed two or three of the fattest of the cows with their spears and roasted the flesh. As soon as it was done, they sacrificed part of the meat to the gods. The rest they fell upon and began to devour.

Odysseus awoke and sniffed the delicious smell. He began to groan, for he guessed what had happened. At once the sun god knew of the outrage that had been done to the golden beasts that were his greatest joy on earth. He went to the throne of Zeus, father of the gods, and asked him to punish with a thunderbolt those who had committed the crime. Thus the punishment of the sailors was assured.

Odysseus, meanwhile, hurried to the place from which came the savoury smell. He bitterly reproached his companions for breaking their oath. But it was too late. They had already begun to feast on the forbidden flesh. Then a strange thing happened. The skins of the slain animals began to creep and writhe, and an unearthly moaning was heard from the lumps of flesh roasting in the fire. Odysseus shook his head sadly. He knew that these were signs of the anger of the gods. For six days he and his crew waited, until the last of the meat was consumed. Then the wind changed, and Odysseus ordered his men to push the ship down to the beach and hoist sail. When all were aboard, they put out to sea, and before long the island was lost to view.

When the ship was in open water, a black cloud appeared overhead. Sea and sky grew dark, until it was impossible to make out which was which. Suddenly the storm struck. The anger of the gods was swift. A hurricane tore the mast from its stays. It crashed down upon the steersman, whose lifeless body rolled into the dark water. The rest of the crew

were washed from the deck. But Odysseus still clung firmly
to what was left of the ship, until it was wholly stripped of
its tackle by the fury of the gale. When the ship was torn to
pieces and the wreckage scattered on the sea, Odysseus
clung to a stout spar and prayed to the gods for deliverance.
He alone, of all the ship's company, had survived the storm.

Then to his horror he saw that once more the wind had changed, and he was being driven helplessly back towards the strait where Scylla and Charybdis lurked. Nearer and nearer he was tossed towards the dreaded whirlpool. Just as the spar to which he clung was about to be sucked into the spinning gulf, he raised himself with all his strength and leaped towards a tree whose branches overhung the pool. There he clung, awaiting death from exhaustion, or deliverance by some miracle sent by the gods. Then the whirlpool subsided for a time, and once more Odysseus saw his fragment of wreckage tossed upon the waters. Hastily ripping part of a branch from the tree to which he was clinging, he sprang into the water and struggled back on to the spar. Then with his home-made paddle he pushed himself as far from the spot as he could, and soon he was once more free of the perils of the strait.

Odysseus was now entirely alone. Across the waves he battled, resolute in his determination to survive all dangers and return to the home he had left so many years before. Just as he was beginning to despair of ever reaching land, he sighted an island. This was the dwelling of the sea-nymph Calypso. He swam ashore and was sighted by Calypso's maidens, who led him to the home of their mistress. Here he was given fresh clothes, food and wine. When he had rested, Odysseus told the nymph all his adventures, and she bade him stay with her till he was ready to continue his journey. He told her he was anxious to set out without delay but Calypso enjoyed the company of the weather-beaten traveller with his endless tales of storm and peril. She entertained him for many months at her palace, with its gardens and vineyards, bright with the song of birds and the glitter of stream and fountain.

At last the gods took a hand. Zeus had determined that Odysseus should reach home after such long and weary travels, so he sent his messenger Hermes to tell the nymph to say good-bye to her guest and speed him on his way.

Accordingly, with sadness in her heart, but obedient to the gods, Calypso gave Odysseus the means to make a raft. She gave him also a favourable wind and bade him farewell. He thanked her for her kindness, hoisted the sail he had made, saw that he had enough provisions for the journey and set out.

But Odysseus had not weathered his last storm. For many days he fared well, and then a sudden squall struck the raft and broke the mast in half. Odysseus and his craft were driven hopelessly hither and thither, with no sail to bear them on. But he did not give up hope, and a sea-nymph, taking pity on his plight, alighted on the raft in the form of a cormorant. She bade him be of stout heart and gave him a girdle. She told him to bind it round himself in case he found it necessary to abandon the raft and take to the water. This girdle would bear him up even in the stormiest of seas. Then the nymph spread her wings and flew off, leaving Odysseus to fare onwards as best the gods would allow.

The Homecoming of Odysseus

Alone on the wide sea, Odysseus was borne along until a storm arose and his raft began to break up. So trusting to the protection of Athene and to the girdle given him by the sea-nymph, he dived into the water. He struggled on until, towards evening, he made out the rocky coast of an island. Half-dead with weariness, he succeeded in scrambling ashore. He gave thanks to the gods for his deliverance, then made himself a bed of dry leaves and fell asleep.

The land where Odysseus was cast up was the island of Scheria, where dwelt a race of sea kings known as the Phaeacians. They were a peaceable people devoted to sailing. Their king was Alcinous, and he ruled his people justly and kindly. On the morning of Odysseus's arrival, his daughter Nausicaa went down to the shore with her maidens and came upon the sleeping hero.

Nausicaa gave Odysseus fresh clothes and brought him back to her father's palace. Here he was given food and wine and was hospitably entertained. But he longed to be on his way, and at last the Phaeacians put him aboard a ship and took him back to his own country of Ithaca. When they reached the harbour, Odysseus was asleep, so they laid him down on the shore and sailed away.

When Odysseus awoke, he had no idea where he was. He

had been away from home for twenty years, and he could not remember what it looked like. But Athene appeared to him in the form of a young shepherd. Odysseus asked the shepherd where he was. The shepherd told him he was in Ithaca, and went on to relate the sorry tale of what had been going on in his absence:

'It is twenty years since our ruler Odysseus left the island to fight in the war against Troy. I was not born then, but my parents have told me everything. Our king left behind his wife, Penelope, and their baby son Telemachus. For ten years the war went on, and ten years have now passed since it ended. But Odysseus has not come home, and not long ago the prince, Telemachus, set off to see if he could get news of his father. For although few suppose him to be alive, no news has yet come of his death.

'About three years ago a great crowd of princes and nobles,

some from Ithaca and some from neighbouring islands, came here and began to seek the hand of the Queen in marriage. So far she has put them off, saying that nothing will make her take another husband, at least until she has proof of Odysseus's death.

'They are rude, unmannerly men, these suitors. They have taken up residence in the city, and daily go and feast at the palace at the Queen's expense. Her best sheep and calves have all been slaughtered and her fields laid waste. Odysseus's old, faithful servants, his herdsmen and reapers, have been insulted and made wretched by the insolent suitors and their followers. In grief and despair Odysseus's mother has died, and his father Laertes has gone to live by himself in a cottage outside the city. The whole land is miserable, and the Queen grieves all day to think of the joyful times before her husband sailed for Troy. All wonder if he will ever return; but as the years go on, hope grows less.

'Daily the suitors become more pressing. They urge her to choose one of them as a husband. She tells them she cannot even think of another husband till she has finished the great cloth she is weaving on her loom. Every day the cloth grows a little, but every night, when all are asleep, she unweaves what she has done during the day. No one can tell how long she can keep the suitors waiting by this trick. Some day they will discover it.'

On hearing this sad story, Odysseus at once began to think how he might be revenged on these insolent visitors. He must not reveal himself, or the suitors would assuredly plot to kill him. So the goddess Athene threw over him the guise of a wretched old beggar, ragged and dirty, and in this guise he set out to see for himself how things were.

When Odysseus was nearing the city, he was kindly received by one of his own old servants. This was the swine-

herd Eumaeus, who lived in a hut and looked after the pigs
belonging to the Queen. His life was made miserable by the
greed and brutality of the suitors. But he remained his old
master's faithful servant.

It was the rule in Ithaca that strangers, even beggars,
should be kindly welcomed, and Eumaeus gave Odysseus
shelter in his hut. He did not know, of course, that it was his
own master he was caring for.

Now it so happened that just at this time Telemachus
returned home from his journey in search of news. He had
visited some of the kings who had returned to their islands
after the fall of Troy. They had told him nothing positive
about his father, except that he had taken a ship from Troy
and set out for home. He had been driven off course, and
little had been seen of him since. Yet none had heard of his
death, and there was a strong feeling that one day he would

return. However, Telemachus dared not show himself openly at the palace for fear the suitors might do him harm. Accordingly the old swineherd Eumaeus was sent to tell Penelope privately of her son's homecoming and see how matters stood at the palace.

As soon as Eumaeus was out of sight and hearing, Athene appeared to Odysseus and told him to reveal himself to his son. Great was the astonishment of the young man to see the ragged beggar transformed into his true self – a vigorous, upstanding and weather-beaten hero. He wept tears of joy on learning that the man was no other than his father, whom he had not seen since he was an infant. Odysseus explained that his disguise was the work of the goddess.

Father and son talked of the important matter of how they were to be revenged on the horde of suitors. Odysseus told Telemachus to return to the palace and mix with the suitors. He was to take his rightful place as head of the household and was to be courteous to strangers and beggars, as had been the custom of old. He was to say nothing of the return of his father. Odysseus, meanwhile, would come to the palace disguised once more as a beggar and would be received in the great hall and be given food and wine. In those days it was customary for wandering beggars to be received in this way, entertaining the great ones in the hall with songs or stories in exchange for their hospitality. Odysseus warned his son that the suitors would insult him and treat him with contempt, but the young man was not to interfere. He must use his father with the respect and courtesy due to any wayfarer, and must not show that he had any special interest in him. In this way the guests would suspect nothing, but simply imagine that Odysseus was an ordinary traveller, begging his way from place to place.

So next morning Telemachus went to the palace and

greeted his mother Penelope. She was overjoyed to see him, as were all the servants, especially Eurycleia, who had been the nurse of Telemachus and of his father before him. Telemachus told Penelope that he had no real news of Odysseus, except that he had been sighted somewhere on his travels and that nowhere had his death been reported. He bade her continue in hope.

Eumaeus, meanwhile, led his guest, the ragged old beggar, to the town. On their way they met a man named Melanthius, who had been Odysseus's goatherd. He was on his way to the palace with the best of the goats, to be slaughtered for the suitors' feast next day. Melanthius was rude to old Eumaeus and insulted the beggar, mocking his raggedness and his hungry looks. Odysseus, who could easily have knocked the goatherd down at a blow, swallowed his insults calmly. He wished no one to suspect that he was no beggar but a man of strength and vigour. But the meeting with the goatherd helped him to see how badly things had gone in Ithaca while he had been away.

When Eumaeus and Odysseus reached the gates of the palace, Eumaeus went inside, to be courteously received by the young master, Telemachus. Odysseus, a little way behind him, noticed an ancient hound, half starved and covered with sores, lying on a dunghill. It was Odysseus's own hound Argus, who had not seen his master for twenty years. But the dog recognised him, raised his head in greeting and wagged his tail. Then he fell back dead. It was as if he had lived only to see once again his beloved master.

When Odysseus reached the door of the great hall, the suitors were gathered at the tables, eating, drinking and laughing together. Telemachus told Odysseus to be seated and sent him a dish of food to eat and a cup of wine. Then he told him that the laws of hospitality allowed him to go boldly from guest to guest asking for money or other gifts.

Odysseus did as his son bade him. Some of the suitors treated him kindly, but Antinous, the boldest and most insolent of them, jeered at them for so treating a mere beggar. Then he picked up a footstool and flung it at the old man. It hit him on the shoulder. Odysseus did nothing, but submitted humbly to the blow. Telemachus, his cheeks reddening, his eyes flashing, longed to avenge this insult offered to the King in his own hall. But he checked himself remembering what his father had told him.

Then Eumaeus took leave of Telemachus and went off to see to the wine. The feasting and revelry continued. Odysseus remained to look after the braziers of live charcoal which had been brought in to warm the suitors after nightfall. Some of the suitors took to insulting the old man, but neither he nor his son answered them. Their taunts only made the thought of revenge the sweeter. The guests

brought out presents for Penelope. She showed herself at the feast, and they urged her to hurry and make up her mind which of them she was going to marry. At length, full of food and wine, the suitors stumbled off to their houses, drunkenly bidding one another good-night and singing snatches of song.

Then Odysseus talked with Penelope, but he dared not yet tell her who he was. He bade her be of good heart and act courageously in the trials before her, for he promised her that Odysseus was living and would suddenly return. She thanked him and wished him good-night, telling the old nurse Eurycleia to see to his needs. Eurycleia took a basin of warm water and a cloth and washed his feet, as was the custom. In so doing, she noticed the scar on one of his legs. She had known it ever since the days when she had had charge of him as a little boy. In her excitement she overturned the bowl of water, and tears came into her eyes. But she said nothing and gave no sign of recognition.

Next day Penelope told her son that he was now old enough to take charge of his own kingdom. She must give up her position as mistress of the palace and decide to choose one or other of the suitors. In this way uncertainty would be ended; she would go off to the home of the winner, so that all the other suitors could be sent away, and peace and order would be restored in Ithaca under the rule of Telemachus. There would be a contest among the suitors for the honour of marrying her. A row of twelve axes was to be set up in the earth floor of the great hall. In the centre of each axe-head was a hole. Then the mighty bow of Odysseus was to be brought out from the place where it had been stored for the past twenty years. Any man who wanted to enter the competition had first to string the bow, then fit an arrow to it and try to shoot it clean through the twelve holes. The first to succeed would be declared the winner.

Next day another feast was prepared, and the suitors came into the great hall and took their places. Once more Odysseus in the guise of a ragged beggar sat at a small table beside the door. Once more he was given food and drink, and once more Antinous and some of the others began to mock at him, throwing him insults and meat bones. Telemachus told them angrily that they must not insult a stranger so long as *he* was master in his own hall. He was now of age and was determined to see that the rules of courtesy were obeyed.

Some of the suitors told the young man that he was quite right to insist on his position as head of the house. But his mother, they said, must keep them waiting no longer and make up her mind which of them she was going to marry.

'We have been kept waiting too long already,' they said. 'She must know that Odysseus will never come back. Let her make up her mind this very day.'

'That she will do this very day,' answered Telemachus. 'She may marry whom she pleases. I will not stop her.'

So when the feasting and drinking were done, Penelope herself, who had been with her servants in the women's quarters, appeared in front of the assembled suitors, bearing in her hands the great bow of Odysseus.

'All who will,' she said, 'may enter the contest for my hand. But the man who marries me must be as strong and valiant as my first husband was. Let each competitor take this bow and bend it. Then let him shoot an arrow at the mark which will now be set up. The strongest and straightest bowman shall be my rightful husband.'

Then Penelope withdrew from the hall, leaving the bow for the suitors to try. They gazed in awe at the mighty weapon which no man had strung for twenty years. The axes were set up in a row, all the blades pointing one way, and the holes at the centre of each axe-head exactly in line.

'Who is to be first to try the bow of the mighty Odysseus?' demanded Telemachus.

A young man stepped forward, grasped the bow and tried to bend it. He failed and was followed by a second one and a third. None could even string the bow, much less aim an arrow through the axes. In the end only Antinous and another of the suitors, Eurymachus, were left. All considered them the strongest of the contestants.

Then Eumaeus and another shepherd, Philoetius, left the feast to go about their work. Odysseus stopped them outside the door of the hall and asked if they were both loyal to their former master. When they said they were, he told them who he was and asked if they were willing to help in the fight against the princes. Both agreed, and Odysseus told them to come back into the hall. There he would himself ask for the bow. The suitors would refuse, but Eumaeus and Philoetius were to give him the bow and then go to the women's quarters and tell them to make fast the doors at the back of the hall, so that no one could escape. Next they were to make fast the main doors.

Then Antinous raised his voice and cried:

'Let us all now go home, and tomorrow we will finish the contest. I and my rival Eurymachus will be fresher tomorrow, and we will try our strength.'

'Before you go, noble sirs,' said Odysseus quietly. 'Let *me* try to bend the bow. I am a poor beggar and have no desire to ask for the hand of Penelope. But once I was sturdy and active, and I would like to see if I have lost all my former strength.'

Some laughed. All stared at the half-starved beggar in rage. Angrily they refused his request. But Telemachus insisted that the old man had a right to try, and Eumaeus took him the bow. While Odysseus was preparing to test his strength, Eumaeus and Philoetius disappeared quietly to do as they had been told, closing and barring all the doors that led from the great hall.

Odysseus then tried the bow and strung it with ease. All marvelled to see the beggar pluck the string and to hear it sing at his touch. Then he picked up an arrow, took aim and sent it hissing through the air. It passed clean through the holes in the line of axes. At this moment Zeus, father of all the gods, sent a sudden clap of thunder as a sign that the hour of Odysseus's vengeance had come. At the same moment the goddess Athene removed from Odysseus the semblance of a beggar and made him appear in his true form – that of a bronzed and handsome warrior in the full vigour of manhood. Seizing a second metal-tipped shaft, he aimed it at Antinous. It went clean through his throat, and

Antinous groaned and fell dead on the floor, blood streaming from the wound.

Before the others could recover from their amazement, Odysseus, standing erect upon the threshold, raised his voice and spoke out in stern and terrifying accents.

'You who have rioted in my palace and laid waste my land – you who seek to carry off my true and lawful wife – know you that Odysseus has returned to his kingdom and that the hour of vengeance has come !'

Eurymachus, who was a coward at heart, began to whine for mercy. He claimed that Antinous, who was now dead, had led them all on. If only Odysseus would have mercy on them, they would depart, leaving him and his country in peace. For answer Odysseus told him they must all pay the full price of their riotous insolence. So Eurymachus told the other suitors they must draw their swords and fight for their lives. Instantly Odysseus fitted another arrow to the bow and shot Eurymachus dead.

Then Telemachus killed with his sword one of the suitors who was trying to flee. There was panic, and on discovering that they could not get out of the hall on account of the barred doors, the suitors determined to fight it out. There were many of them against Odysseus and his three loyal comrades – Telemachus, Eumaeus and Philoetius.

Things began to look black for them, when the goddess Athene appeared in the person of Mentor, an old companion whom Odysseus had left in charge of his household when he departed for Troy. Odysseus appealed to Mentor, who promised help and bade the hero be of stout heart. Then the goddess flew off in the form of a swallow, to light on one of the rafters overhead. The battle went on. Telemachus and Eumaeus were wounded. Despite this, the courage and fury of the defenders, aided by the goddess, were redoubled. Panic seized the suitors, who tried vainly to escape. In the crush all were slain. Bloody but victorious, Odysseus and his comrades were in possession of the hall, the palace and the kingdom.

The delight of Penelope on being reunited with her husband can scarcely be imagined. It was Eurycleia, the old nurse, who broke the news of her husband's return and of his victory over the hated princes. Next day they went to tell the almost unbelievable story to Laertes, Odysseus's father. The old man could scarcely speak for joy and astonishment.

Thus Odysseus and his family were brought together again in peace and happiness after the trials of the Trojan war and the perilous adventures of the long voyage home.